The Challenge Of

BANGLA DESH

A SPECIAL DEBATE

Edited by

PRAN CHOPRA

**NEW YORK
HUMANITIES PRESS**

First published in United States of America 1971

PRINTED IN INDIA

PRINTED BY MANMOHAN S. BHATKAL AT POPULAR BOOK DEPOT (PRINTING DIVISION)
SHIVAJI SERVICE INDUSTRIAL ESTATE, TAIKALWADI ROAD, MAHIM, BOMBAY 16 AND
PUBLISHED BY HUMANITIES PRESS, 303, PARK AVENUE SOUTH 10017
NEW YORK N.E.

ACKNOWLEDGEMENTS BY
COMBAT

WRITERS, artists, and men of the professions who have joined to form COMBAT thank all those who have donated time, talent and material to the making of this book. In particular, they thank:

The scholars and journalists who have written for this book without taking royalties.

Pran Chopra who has edited the book, Gopi Gajwani who has designed the lay-out and the jacket and Uma Anand who has read the proofs free of charge.

The printer, publisher and distributor who have given up a substantial part of their profits.

Karamchand Thapar & Bros. (Private) Ltd., New Delhi, who have donated the paper.

The Tribune, Chandigarh, *The Assam Tribune,* Gauhati, *The Hindustan Standard,* Calcutta, *The Sandesh,* Ahmedabad, and other newspapers which carry Pran Chopra's syndicated column and have allowed the use of some of his articles in portions of the Introduction, especially the following:

"Where Do We Go From Saying Nothing?"	... ...	Published on 16, April 1971.
"A Problem of Guts And Credibility"	... ...	" 25, April 1971.
"Pakistan Turns The Table on India"	... ...	" 14, May 1971.
"Rights For Refugees, Not Charity"	... ...	" 21, May 1971.
"Between Hopes And Illusions"	... ...	" 4, June 1971.

CONTRIBUTORS

PRAN CHOPRA is political commentator and former Editor of *The Statesman*, Calcutta and New Delhi.

SISIR GUPTA is Professor of Diplomacy at the Indian School of International Studies, Jawaharlal Nehru University, New Delhi.

MOHAMMED AYOOB is Assistant Professor of Pakistani Studies at the Indian School of International Studies, Jawaharlal Nehru University, New Delhi.

COL. R. RAMA RAO (Rtd.) and BRIG. RATHY SAWHNY (Rtd.) are members of the staff of the Indian Institute of Defence Studies and Analyses, New Delhi.

ARJUN SENGUPTA, DR. is Reader in Economics at the Delhi School of Economics and was formerly Lecturer at the London School of Economics.

V. P. DUTT, DR. is Pro-Vice-Chancellor and Professor of Chinese Studies, Delhi University.

DEWAN BERINDRANATH is a journalist with a special interest in the affairs of West Pakistan.

The three American economists whose statement appears as an Appendix are:

EDWARD S. MASON, Lamont University, Professor EMERITUS at Harvard University and formerly director of the team which drew up the first development programme for Pakistan.

ROBERT DORFMAN, Professor of Economics at Harvard University and formerly member of a team appointed by President Kennedy in 1961 at the request of President Ayub Khan to advise the Government of Pakistan.

STEPHEN A. MARGLIN, Professor of Economics at Harvard University and at various times adviser to various governments in Asia, Africa, and Latin America and the United States, the World Bank and United Nations.

CONTENTS

THE STAKES FOR INDIA

PRAN CHOPRA

THE EXPLOSION witnessed in East Bengal has been in the making ever since Pakistan came into being. Or indeed, since before. As Sisir Gupta explains in his illuminating survey, while Pakistan was as yet an idea, East Bengal had misgivings about its place in the country which was yet to be. The leaders of East Bengal constantly asked the central leadership of the Muslim League what would be the relations of their half of the country with the rest of it, because at the very inception of Pakistan they had reason to be anxious about the danger of domination by non-Bengali Muslims. The founding document of the concept of Pakistan, the resolution passed by the Muslim League at Lahore in 1940, spoke of the north western and north eastern regions of India, later the two wings of Pakistan, as "independent states" and of their constituent units as "autonomous and sovereign". But the mover of the resolution, the East Bengal leader, Fazlul Haq, himself resigned only a year later because he feared that the interests of his region would not be looked after by the leaders of the Muslim League. His fears were amply justified: far from being allowed to be "autonomous and sovereign", East Bengal was denied a due share

1

of power even in a centralised system; it contributed the greater part of the population and economic resources of Pakistan but counted for very little at the seat of the national authority.

Scholars have given sociological explanations for this denial of its rights to East Bengal, the denial of the rights of a majority by an oligarchical clique which wholly belonged to the western wing. The compelling reason is said to be the cultural gap between the two wings. This gap may have been a contributory reason, but the more basic reason was the dictatorial nature of the ruling West Pakistani coterie and the power of the mailed fist which was given to it—in the name of democracy!—by the United States and Great Britain. Whether civilian, so long as Ghulam Mohammad was the Governor-General, or part civilian and part military under the non-martial General Iskander Mirza or purely military under Generals Ayub Khan and Yahya Khan, the regime remained dictatorial in effect even if from time to time it took some democratic half steps. It did not let democracy grow even in West Pakistan, though the area is culturally much more homogeneous than India is. After the mysterious assassination of the only more or less democratically inclined Prime Minister Pakistan has ever had, Liaquat Ali Khan, democracy was allowed to perish at the hands of politicians who played musical chairs with it. Their behaviour was indeed abominable and their misrule had to be ended. But the appeal should have been to the electorate. There was as good a chance in Pakistan as in India at a corresponding stage that the people would have thrown up a responsible new leadership. But this was not acceptable to the ruling oligarchy. It was less interested in how power was exercised than in who exercised it. Therefore, while claiming for a time that it had seized power only to make Pakistan safe for democracy, it only perpetuated its dictatorial rule, which it made as absolute in one wing as in the other. Until elections were held throughout the country last year to choose a national assembly for framing a new constitution, they had been held only once in the eastern wing and never in the western.

The ruling oligarchy as firmly opposed democratic aspirations in East Bengal as it was later to oppose the demand for greater autonomy. As Sisir Gupta shows, under the popular leadership of Fazlul Haq and Suhrawardy, East Bengal elected a new government in 1954 by a convincing majority. But it was not allowed to hold office for long: just as the oligarchy deposed the political government at the centre by engineering riots in Lahore, it also overthrew the popularly elected government in Dacca after inciting a riot at Narayanganj. Thereafter no popular government was allowed to hold office in any part of Pakistan; only a succession of dictators ruled the country from Karachi or Islamabad. An intense popular agitation first softened up and then overthrew the dictatorship of Ayub Khan, which had become at least relatively benign towards its end. But only another West Pakistani dictatorship followed, as Mohammed Ayoob explains. This made East Bengal's later demand for autonomy both just and inevitable.

A country as diverse as Pakistan, with its two wings separated by 1,200 miles of alien territory, could not have been held together under the highly centralised rule of a handful of persons. Dictatorial cliques always consist of tightly knit coteries; they are usually identified with a dominant but very narrow class or group or area. Other areas or groups and classes are thus alienated from the centre of power and have to be held down by force whether it is implied or explicit. But in a democratic system, with authority vested in a large, wide-based and popularly elected assembly, all classes and areas of the country can find at least some reflection of themselves at the seat of central authority, which thus becomes more acceptable to them. If Pakistan had been ruled by a popularly elected legislature with each part represented in it according to its population, East Bengal would have had the share of power which the majority of a country's population has the right to expect. It would not have become, and what is as important in politics, it would not have felt that it had become a majority exploited by a clique on behalf of an alien minority.

But convinced by its own experience that a popularly elected authority would never be allowed to rule at the centre, and angered by the colonialistic exploitation of its economy by the west, which has been analysed by Arjun Sengupta, East Bengal was gradually driven to the view that either it must have autonomy to be able to look after its interests within Pakistan—or else it must fight for its independence. The last chance for steering it away from such a course was lost when President Yahya Khan reneged on his own promises and refused

3

to let the National Assembly meet though it had been elected under his own auspices. To the Awami League of Sheikh Mujibur Rehman, which had swept the polls in East Bengal, and to East Bengal itself which for the first time had acquired the majority of the seats in a national body because it was chosen on the basis of one-man-one-vote, this was final proof that the oligarchical rump in Islamabad, which belonged entirely to the western wing and only to a narrow segment thereof as Berindranath explains, would never allow justice to be done to East Bengal. Thereafter events inevitably led to the tragic hostilities which broke out on the night between March 25-26 this year.

Throughout these developments, India faced a situation which was difficult at its best and at its worst most cruel. Her interests were being sucked in by the vortex of Pakistan's domestic and external politics, but she could do little to protect them. Especially events in East Bengal affected her closely; but she could do little to control or even influence them. Almost the day Pakistan was born, the most popular leaders of East Bengal began to be accused by the rulers of Pakistan of conspiring with India. These charges were made against Suhrawardy in 1948, against Fazlul Haq in 1954 and against Sheikh Mujibur Rehman—the most popular and famous among them—and he was framed up in what came to be known as the Agartala conspiracy case. In no instance were the charges proved to the satisfaction of even such courts as were allowed to function under the successive dictatorships. But they were used as the pretext for frustrating the verdict of the people. The clearer the verdict, the more ruthlessly it was overturned, as a comparison between the events of 1954 and 1971 shows: in 1954, only the government was deposed; in 1971, when Mujibur Rehman and his Awami League won nearly all the East Bengal seats, the whole people were sought to be bludgeoned into disowning him and his party.

But that only widened the gap between the western and eastern wings' attitudes towards India, making India a party to the controversy against her wishes. Although East Bengal was as badly infected with the communal virus as West Pakistan—as badly as many parts of India, too—it never allowed hatred of India to become a conditioned reflex, as it became in the western wing. It always considered Pakistan's hostility towards

4

India a special condition of the West Pakistan mind and Karachi's or Islamabad's overwhelming preoccupation with Kashmir as a vested interest of the military regime. But this negative difference developed into a more positive one as the western wing intensified its repression and exploitation of East Bengal. First a desire for closer economic cooperation with India began to be more openly expressed; next a desire for contacts on a wider cultural front, especially with West Bengal; and finally India was urged to intervene and help when the West Pakistan army let loose its terror in March this year. Not only the Provisional Government of Bangla Desh but also the pro-Peking leader, Maulana Bhashani, openly turned towards India in the following May. On the other hand the western wing became even more aggressively hostile towards India with the passage of time. The overpowering desire to get even with India for the loss of Kashmir became the sole motivation behind the ordering of the central government's priorities. This push and pull combination made India an involuntary and at the same time helpless party to the inter-wing dispute. The old adage that your enemy's enemy is your friend added to other causes of sympathy between India and East Bengal. But at this level the dispute remained essentially an internal affair of Pakistan; it did not directly impinge upon India.

But at another level it did, as V. P. Dutt explains. Taking its cue from Britain, the United States also began to use Pakistan as a counterpoise to India. The more obvious reasons why it did so are not relevant here. Indo-Soviet relations were one of them. India's non-alignment another. A third quite clearly arose from India's geo-political situation which made it plain that far from being willing to play a subordinate role, India would one day become an independent centre of some importance in this part of the world unless it was curbed in time; this idea of curbing a possible Indian role later became the central drive of Sino-Pak relations, and it is possible to suspect that it also played a part in Soviet diplomacy. But a more complex part of American thinking intricately linked up Pakistan's internal and inter-wing dispute with West Pakistan's running hot and semi-hot war with India. From then on Pakistan's "internal affairs" began to impinge heavily upon India's interests.

Though actively and vigorously democratic at home, the United States has not been partial to democracies in choosing its allies abroad, especially in Asia. From Seoul southwards and westwards it has almost consistently rejected the democratic alternative and chosen the authoritarian. This has not been a matter of local chance and contingency but directly flows from America's overall view of the Asian reality. Like the rest of interested American opinion, Washington has always been sceptical of the stability and effectiveness of democratic institutions in Asian conditions. On 18 May this year, the US Assistant Secretary of State for Near Eastern and South Asian Affairs, Joseph Sisco, paid a handsome tribute to the workings of democracy in India. But the view which held sway in the State Department before that was expressed by William Bundy, for a long time Sisco's predecessor in the Department. Writing in *Newsweek* of 10 May, he expressed agreement with the doubts of "many scholars of Asia" about Asian elections because "the traditions of Asia, derived from China and India for the most part, tend to a tremendous respect for authority and for hierarchy—that is, an established order in which the positions of superior and inferior are defined. Unity comes way ahead of liberty in the classic struggle of values......" An authoritarian regime is much more able to deliver the goods in this view than one which democratically tries to accommodate all the diversities which make up the pluralistic nations of Asia. So, just as American policy-makers chose to back Pakistan in southern Asia instead of, if not even against, India, they also chose the authoritarian rulers of West Pakistan. And, as Sisir Gupta explains, they did so in a manner which made them allies of the military regime against the struggling democrats of East Bengal.

Because of this background, as Pakistan, which in this context means West Pakistan, became more and more involved in the global diplomacy of the United States, it set in motion two simultaneous and parallel processes. By one, the status of East Bengal in Pakistan began to deteriorate very rapidly; by the other, Indian interests began to be impinged upon very severely and directly. American aid made it easier for the military regime to displace the primacy of politics which is natural in a democracy. In any political regime, especially if it was also democratic, East Bengal would have had the majority share of power in proportion to its population, and such a regime would not have been hostile to India. But Pakistan's hostility and the political deprivation of East Bengal increased hand in hand as American backing added to the ascendency of the military oligarchy from the early 'fifties. Later, more or less the same thing happened when Pakistan's relations with the Soviet Union and China developed. Both in the competitive and cooperative phases of the overlap between American and Russian diplomacy in this part of the world, the military oligarchy of West Pakistan gained at the expense of both East Bengal and India, and it gained some more when it succeeded in playing off both the United States and the Soviet Union against China. Specifically, it acquired teeth, which it used against India unsuccessfully but against East Bengal with devastating effect, inflicting terrible losses upon the civilian population and economic assets of the eastern wing. How successful the West Pakistan army will be in retaining its grip upon Bangla Desh is a different matter; its chances have been discussed at length by Col. Rama Rao and Brig. Sawhny. But the immediate effect of its attack has been to suck Indian interests still more deeply into this vortex.

To some extent West Pakistan has, unwittingly, benefited India. By so ruthlessly suppressing half of its own population, Pakistan has destroyed such competence as it may have ever had to speak for the rights of the people of Kashmir. It may yet accuse India of not holding elections under the auspices of the United Nations. But it cannot deny that it has forcibly overturned even the results of elections held under its own auspices; military retribution has been visited upon those who swept the polls in East Bengal, and the National Assembly in which they would have had the majority has not been allowed to meet. The Kashmiris at least have the satisfaction that they are fully represented in proportion to their population both in the state legislature and in the Union Parliament. Pakistan has also destroyed, at least for a long time if not for ever, the use it might have had in American or Chinese diplomacy as a counterpoise to India or in Russian diplomacy as a companion country to be wooed simultaneously with India. These countries may still try to use Pakistan, as they have done in the past, as a rival or as a parallel force in southern Asia. But they will be even less successful in making it so than they

7

were in the past. Whether West Pakistan succeeds in conquering Bangla Desh or not, it has severely damaged its power potential. To that extent—and in that sense only—it has also ceased to be a threat to India's security; except as a desperate gamble by a reckless or panicky junta in Islamabad, Pakistan cannot repeat in the foreseeable future the kind of attacks it launched upon India in 1947 and 1965. If it tries, the consequences will be far worse for it.

But it has also done considerable damage to essential Indian interests, and it has created a very different but nevertheless very serious threat to India's security. At the time of writing, more than four million refugees have already poured into India, and they are still coming in at such a rate that the number can rise by a million every fortnight. This has very serious implications for India, both immediate and in the long run. Within less than two months of the beginning of the influx, the economy of the two states which are bearing the brunt, Assam and West Bengal, had been severely affected. Even the national economy had suffered to such an extent that some of the welfare programmes which the ruling party had begun to take up in response to the pledges it made at the time of the elections had to be modified or given up. For the most minimal programme of refugee relief, India may have to spend more every day in the course of June and July than West Pakistan will then be spending on military operations in Bangla Desh. Before long India will certainly have spent more on this item than on the whole of its military operation in 1965, in which she blunted Pakistan's offensive capability for many years to come.

More serious is the security threat which India might face as a result of political conditions which can be created by the armed suppression of the popular movement for Bangla Desh. Movements of this kind turn more radical in such circumstances. People do not accept defeat; they only turn to other methods. Conditions in the whole of this region are such—not only in eastern India and Bangla Desh but also in northern Burma and further afield—that an acutely radical movement in any part of it can open up opportunities for outside subversion in the whole area. A certain amount of internal support for such subversion has existed in the area for a long time, and in India's democratic conditions, political stability can be the only real answer to it. Chances of containing it became much brighter in March 1971 when the Indian political system not only displayed its ability to become stable again after a period of turmoil but also proved the value of the ballot-box in mobilising the reformative power of discontents. But the forcible thwarting of this power just across the border weakens the instructive value of the Indian example, while at the same time creating a base of operations for discontended radicals. The danger of communalism may also raise threats to India's security as the influx of refugees drastically alters the demographic balance in India's eastern states either between linguistic or religious communities or both. It can be taken for granted that many among those whom the West Pakistan army has pushed into India are "planted" refugees who will try to inflame the communal sutures on this side of the border. The whole region may be thrown into confusion, and it is too much to expect that China would not seek to take advantage of it—and on both sides of the border. Hitherto it has sided with West Pakistan; but this may be only a watching position, pending a final assessment of what use it can make of the situation as it further develops.

More intangible, but not for that reason less serious, is the damage India's standing may suffer in this region. The contrast between what the consequences are for India and what they would have been if the Bangla Desh movement had succeeded more quickly is too glaring not to have been noticed by India's neighbours and other countries of southern Asia. They know that the people of East Bengal have long desired closer economic cooperation with India, and that with such cooperation India and East Bengal can find much better answers to the grave economic and political problems of the area than either can by itself. Therefore these countries would have thought that India would do more to help Bangla Desh than merely pass a resolution in Parliament or issue other sympathetic statements or distribute dole among the refugees. Some of them might have been impressed by India's refusal to intervene in the affairs of a neighbour. But the more likely reaction of others must have been to question India's credibility as a power factor in the area; they would regard India's non-interventionism as passivity enforced by the fear of displeasure which a more positive policy by her would cause in Peking or some other capital.

There is an interesting contrast for them between India's inactivity and the more adventurous courses followed by Pakistan. Taking advantage of the excuse presented by discontented Kashmiris, a minute number compared with the people of East Bengal who not only constitute the majority of the population of Pakistan but clearly declared their opposition to the Islamabad regime, Pakistan twice mounted full-scale attacks on India and in between constantly kept up harassing raids across the Indian frontier. In the present case also West Pakistan decisively and swiftly intervened from three thousand miles away, defying all the laws of logistical caution, and despite the condemnation by public opinion in nearly all parts of the world, firmly pushed in the sword all the way to the hilt. On the other hand India allowed Pakistan, as Mrs. Gandhi lamented, to convert its own crisis into a serious problem for her. What India could have done may not be very clear to interested observers. But they must consider it significant that she did very little, making them suspect that either she cannot see or cannot save her friends. This has certainly been the reaction of large sections of the Indian population, to the detriment of the widespread impression that Mrs. Gandhi's election had given India a decisive and effective leadership.

There are certain circumstances which place India's inactivity in a better light. Right upto the beginning of March this year, the Government of India believed, as did Sheikh Mujibur Rehman and the Awami League too, that Yahya Khan sincerely desired to hand over power to a constitutional government elected by the people. This hope ran counter to certain basic compulsions of the military regime, which are analysed by Mohammed Ayoob. But it was expected that the shock of popular protest which had overthrown President Ayub, who until then had appeared to be imperishable, had convinced the oligarchy which was ruling Pakistan that it was no longer possible to deny the normal powers of a democracy to the people. It was further thought that the sweeping victories scored by anti-establishment parties in both wings in the elections in 1970, Bhutto's People's Progressive Party in West Pakistan and the Awami League in the East, had further burnt this lesson into the minds of the rulers in Islamabad. Yahya Khan certainly appeared to be acting as though it had; his personal inclination was also thought to be to achieve the distinction of being the first military ruler ever to abdicate voluntarily in favour of the people.

The prospect was very pleasing to New Delhi. Contrary to the belief held in West Pakistan, responsible opinion in India, especially official, has always been that it is better to have a stable than an unstable neighbour in Pakistan, provided only that it gives up its attitude of permanent hostility to India and quits laying claims on Kashmir. It was expected that such a Pakistan would result from any viable settlement Yahya Khan made with the Awami League because he would either have to concede large scale autonomy to East Bengal or give it a very substantial say in the central government of Pakistan. In the former event Pakistan would not be able, in the latter event not anxious, to persist in hostile neighbourliness. In either event it would abandon the ambition to become the counterpoise to India which western diplomacy had tried to make it in the past; the Soviet policy, discussed by V. P. Dutt, of trying to carry both India and Pakistan in a triangular relationship would also become far more acceptable to New Delhi than it had been. In New Delhi's eyes this was such a welcome scenario that perhaps a little wishful thinking went into the estimates which were made of the likely outcome of the political initiatives taken by Yahya Khan, especially in letting the country hold its first ever nation-wide elections. The result was that the decision-makers in India were caught quite unprepared for the consequences of the somersault which Yahya Khan took when, without any warning to or consultation with Sheikh Mujibur Rehman, whom he had described as the future Prime Minister of Pakistan, he abruptly cancelled the inaugural meeting of the newly elected National Assembly which he had himself fixed for 3 March 1971.

By about the middle of March it began to be clear that there would be no transfer of power, and about ten days later that instead there would be intense and prolonged repression in East Bengal. But even then thoughts of an Indian role were inhibited by two mutually contradictory expectations. First, an exaggerated impression was formed of what the liberation movement would be able to do on its own, without outside assistance, in frustrating the onslaught of the West Pakistan army. Indian opinion was obviously impressed by the logistical and other difficulties the military regime in Islamabad would face in suppressing a popular movement of this magnitude three thousand miles away and in the midst of an entirely hostile population. But it did not take into account the ruthlessness the regime would show in benumbing the movement through the shock of terror. It is quite clear in retrospect that India did not appreciate in time how uninhibited a military dictatorship can be in using force, especially against a culturally alien population even if it is a part of the nation. Second, it was thought that other countries would be much more active than they turned out to be in restraining the military regime. Since one of the reasons why Pakistan occupied such an important place in the diplomatic calculations of both the Soviet Union and the United States was that they did not want China's domination over it, it was thought very unlikely that the two super powers would not use, or would not be effective in using, their very considerable leverage in Islamabad to prevent it from persisting in a course which would certainly make China's influence over it even stronger than it already was. It was obvious to India, and she thought it would be obvious to other countries too, that repressed anger in East Bengal would create ideal conditions for China. The firmness of the Soviet President's note to Yahya Khan reinforced this hope. But in the event, the first hope fizzled out very quickly; the second gave only fitful evidence of turning out to be true—some day.

Authoritative comment warning against these hopes was not lacking in India. It was pointed out that even if the Awami League had been much better prepared than it was for the turn which events took, it would have needed substantial outside assistance to force at least an expensive stalemate if not a defeat upon the powerfully equipped West Pakistan army. It was argued, as Col. Rama Rao does, that liberation movements had rarely succeeded without such help even where combativeness was more matched than it is between the average East Bengali and West Pakistani. What intervention, however informal, would cost India, whether in terms of money or diplomatic complications was not overlooked or understated; but it was considered to be much less than the cost in terms of India's credibility and in terms of the financial and political burden of a large scale influx of refugees, which was clearly predicted. As May drew to an end and the conflict in Bangla Desh entered the third month, the warning proved to be more accurate than the hopes. But hopes persist. At least official statements are still optimistic.

Since about the middle of May, the Prime Minister, Mrs. Gandhi, has been saying with some confidence that in about six months' time the refugees will be able to go back to their homes in East Bengal. The basis of this hope has never been clearly divulged, but it has been communicated to the team sent by the United Nations Commissioner for Refugees, which is also proceeding on the basis, according to its public statements, that international relief operations may not be needed beyond the end of this year. They too are silent about their reasons for these calculations. It is possible that the reasons are nothing more substantial than the thought that it is good to have a deadline in mind; countries which are promising refugee relief might be scared off by the prospects of an unending commitment. But it is not impossible that the optimism takes colour from factors which government sources can see more clearly than the ordinary public.

Foremost among them is the possibility that governments which have been the main source of military and economic aid to Pakistan, especially the United States and the Soviet Union, do mean it when they privately convey the impression that they will not give Pakistan any more aid until Islamabad agrees to take back the refugees and—although their hints about this are very ambiguous—makes a reasonable political settlement with East Bengal. Next only to the fortunes of battle on the ground, the hopes of Bangla Desh lie in either the economic strain or the political repercussions which may follow from it in West Pakistan becoming too severe for Islamabad to handle. Responsible people in New Delhi believe that the United States and the World Bank do intend to apply economic pressure upon Islamabad. They give credence to the report in the *New York Times* in the third week of May that while the United States and Britain were willing to organise substantial aid for Pakistan, they would do so only after Islamabad met these two conditions. Other aid-giving countries such as Japan, France, Sweden and Pakistan's nearer neighbours in West Asia have not so far given similar indications. But some are believed to be not acquainted with all the facts as yet. Hence the diplomatic drive which India began in the middle of May to explain all the facts to countries which are believed to be open to conviction (only the Arab countries, and of course Britain, are suspected to have a closed mind on this).

Apart from political expectations, there is impartial scholarly backing for the belief that Pakistan is most vulnerable on the economic front. In the course of a debate in ECOSOC on 12 May, Pakistan's representative, Agha Shahi, charged the eastern aid-giving countries, the World Bank and the Harvard School of Economists with equal responsibility for the "exploitation of East Pakistan." If Islamabad ever suspected these sources of deliberately setting up an economic system which was unfavourable to East Bengal, it must have been a very willing accomplice; East Bengal economists laid bare the colonialist nature of this system a long time ago. Shahi's anger against the Harvard School and the World Bank was probably a reaction to a document, reproduced here as an appendix, which three American economists circulated within a week of the West Pakistan army's attack upon Bangla Desh. Arjun Sengupta presents a more detailed analysis of the economic argument. But the credentials of the authors of this document make their comments especially noteworthy. They had the opportunity to study Pakistan's economy very closely. One of them, Edward S. Mason, was director of a team of eight specialists who advised Pakistan on its first development plan; another, Robert Dorfman, was a member of an advisory team appointed by President Ayub Khan in 1961; the third, Stephen A. Marglin, has at various times advised different governments in Asia, Africa and Latin America, as well as the World Bank and the United Nations. With these credentials they prepared a statement on the prospects in Pakistan which, in its summary, starts with the sentence "The independence of East Pakistan is inevitable".

But any expectation that economic strain or political tension in West Pakistan will drive Islamabad to a political settlement with East Bengal and to taking back all the refugees would be, to say the least, premature and unrealistic in the light of all the known facts. There is endless room for prevarication by Islamabad in terms like "settlement" and "refugees", and there is no firm evidence of sufficient clarity of purpose or perseverance in Washington or Moscow which would force Islamabad not to play with words. There are signs of strain in West Pakistan which support the economic analysis of Arjun Sengupta and the political forecast by Berindranath; the latter is especially well supported by the statements Bhutto made in the middle of May and Abdul Qayum Khan on 20 May, both asking for replacement of military rule by constitutional and political rule, and by the resignation of Wali Khan, chairman of NAP, the second biggest party in West Pakistan, in protest against the severe curbs on political activity. But neither Bhutto nor Abdul Qayum Khan nor Wali Khan is a trusted defender of the interests of East Bengal! The persecution of the Awami League will not abate by any means if power in Islamabad passes into their or similar hands. As for a political regime in East Bengal, it is too much to expect that Yahya Khan will not be able to put together a quisling rump with the aid of some of the elements which have been helping the regime in tracking down freedom fighters; once it is installed in Dacca, he would be able to contrast it well with the present extent of the control of Mukti Fouj, which is pitiably small in any demonstrable terms despite growing signs that its will to resist is durable.

As for taking back the refugees, Yahya Khan has already raised several terminological stumbling blocks. Possibly in deference to the Soviet Union and the United States Yahya Khan issued a statement on 21 May inviting the refugees to return. But the statement is riddled with qualifications which can lead to endless hair splitting. "Law abiding citizens of Pakistan...." he said were free to return. But by a twist of definition all those who fled East Bengal can be described as not law abiding because they ran away from their "normal duties". With what evidence would the refugees be required to convince the border authorities of the regime that they were "citizens of Pakistan" and not "the unemployed and homeless people of West Bengal" who, Yahya Khan has already alleged, are being counted as refugees by India in order to present an "inflated" figure to the world? In another part of the statement Yahya Khan made the ominous allegation that a large number of Muslims had been driven out of India since 1964, that India had "refused to take them back", and that he hoped India would fulfil its "obligations" in this regard. The allegation is ominous because this may only be the tip of the iceberg of the controversy he can raise over the repatriation of refugees. The trail of the refugee traffic in both directions goes so far back that once anyone begins to trace it he can lose track of the cause of Bangla Desh.

In the meantime many more months can pass than the six stipulated in the recent India statements. A sizeable number of refugees will not be able to cross this semantic barrier unless a government comes into being in Dacca which recognises them as its people.

Therefore the challenge of Bangla Desh will not be met at the tables of the checking staff which may be set up on the borders of East Bengal. It will be met only if Islamabad accepts and implements, or is made to, the verdict of the elections held in 1970 in which the Awami League unquestionably proved itself to be the sole representative of the people of Bangla Desh. If the super powers show a strong enough conviction about the value of democratic institutions even in Asian conditions, they can successfully undertake this task of the moral enforcement of a popular verdict. But if they do not, India will face the same difficult options at the end of this year as it faced in the middle. The passage of time may not be found to have made them easier to face.

FROM THE PARTITION TO YAHYA KHAN

A Political Survey

SISIR GUPTA

THE UNPRECEDENTED courage shown in Bangla Desh should rouse the conscience of the world to the right of self-determination of a nation of 75 million people. They have been subjected to colonial rule and exploitation by a power-mad minority which has built up an authoritarian pattern of government even in the metropolitan area, that is West Pakistan. Now that they have risen in revolt against it, they are being crushed by the brutal military assault of a minority upon the majority. The world in general and the new nations of Asia and Africa in particular have rightly asserted the principle that the right of self-determination cannot be extended to sub-national groups lest it should bring about a colossal change in the states system evolved in the post-war years. But East Bengal was never a sub-nation. Not only does it form the majority of the population of Pakistan; history has shaped it into a distinct national identity. The nationalism of East Bengal which lay dormant in the minds of the people in the early years after the partition has taken shape in response to the colonial domination and exploitation of their land by the ruling elite of West Pakistan.

Interestingly, one of the Afro-Asian states which has continuously insisted on self-determination for a sub-national group within another state is Pakistan. The striking resemblance between the attitudes of some imperialist powers and those of Pakistan on the question of the integrity of new nations is not accidental. In both cases the encouragement to sub-national and separatist groups within other societies is a device for diverting attention from their own imperial stranglehold over peoples with whom they have little in common. Indeed, Pakistan's claim that East Bengal is its province is in some ways comparable to the claim Portugal once laid upon Goa: a dictatorial regime in the metropolitan country has used the argument of religious affinity to bolster its claim to colonial domination over a distinct and different people.

In order to understand the difference between what is happening in Bangla Desh today and the sub-national urges which have found expression in other countries of the world, one has to look at the history of Pakistan and to analyse the structure of this absurd state. Long before the All-India Muslim League accepted the Pakistan resolution, the idea of creating a separate state in the Indian sub-continent was propounded by the poet-philosopher, Iqbal. But he only envisaged a state of the Muslims of the north-western provinces of India. In his view they needed a separate state not only because they were Muslims but also because they were north-westerners. The early enthusiasts of Pakistan, like the group of students in Cambridge who brought out a pamphlet in 1934 to suggest the creation of a separate state in the sub-continent, had also a similar north-western Indian state in mind. In fact that word PAKISTAN was explained by them as an anagram made up of P from Punjab, A from Afghanistan, K from Kashmir, S from Sind and TAN from Baluchistan.

Unlike Iqbal and the Cambridge group, Jinnah sought a homeland for all Indian Muslims. His political capital was the Indo-Muslim consciousness and his political outlook was all-Indian largely because of the nature of the All-India Muslim League. It was a party of the Muslims of the Muslim minority areas, not a party of the Muslims of Punjab, Sind, Baluchistan and the North-West Frontier Province, not to speak of East Bengal. The Muslim elite of U.P., Bihar and Bombay had an overwhelming voice in the articulation of Muslim aspirations in Indian society. It is not surprising, therefore, that to the All-India

Muslim League, Iqbal's concept of Pakistan had little appeal. They were not interested in a separate homeland for the Muslims of north-western India; they wanted to manipulate the Indo-Muslim consciousness, later articulated in the form of the two-nation theory, to secure for all the Muslims of India, particularly the Muslims of the minority areas, a higher status than they could have acquired only through democratic principles.

It is questionable whether the All-India Muslim League ever seriously wanted an independent Pakistan. It is interesting to note that the League readily accepted the Cabinet Mission Plan of 1946 which promised to create a loose confederal structure in India in which the two Muslim majority areas would, along with princely India, be able to dominate a central government. However, events overtook the Muslim League and it found itself in August, 1947, to be the ruler of a Pakistan which defied the logic of nationhood. In substituting his concept of Pakistan for Iqbal's, Jinnah created an impossible problem of identity for the new state—a problem of identity which successive governments tried to resolve in terms of a nationalism based on religion and sustained by unabated hostility towards India. But religion proved to be inadequate as the basis of nationalism, and the process of modernisation which began in Pakistan shortly after independence made it still more inadequate. Political and economic developments in Pakistan made it impossible to unify the two wings, East and West Pakistan.

The problems of the national identity of Pakistan were largely the problems of the structure of a geographically absurd state hastily created by the British before their withdrawal from India in 1947. More than 55 per cent of the people of Pakistan lived in East Bengal, whereas the seats of political and economic power and authority lay in West Pakistan. And the two were separated by one thousand miles of Indian territory. The distance between Lahore and Dacca is the distance between London and Warsaw and more than the distance between Rangoon and Kunming or that between Dar-es-Salaam and Lusaka. The people of the two wings of Pakistan are different from each other in race and culture. Their languages are very different; so are their scripts. The climatic conditions in the two wings of Pakistan are poles apart. Economically, the majority of the Pakistani people who live in East Pakistan are

19

worse off than the minority which lives in West Pakistan; the per capita income in West Pakistan is nearly double of that in East Pakistan. East Pakistan earns most of the foreign exchange whereas West Pakistan spends most of it. The elite in East Pakistan is drawn from small-scale farming families whereas the elite in West Pakistan is drawn from the families of large-scale farmers, landlords and feudal masters.

The founding fathers of Pakistan foresaw the problems of a common state and government for the two areas and the Lahore resolution of 1940, which demanded Pakistan, was utterly vague on the question of the status of the two Muslim majority areas of the Indian sub-continent in a future constitutional set-up. The resolution stated:

"No constitutional plan would be workable in this country or acceptable to Muslims unless it is designed on the following basic principle, namely, that geographical contiguous units are demarcated into regions which should be constituted with such territorial readjustments as may be necessary, that the areas in which the Muslims are numerically in a majority, as in the north western and eastern zones of India, should be grouped to constitute 'Independent States' in which the constituent units shall be autonomous and sovereign."

The unexpected and somewhat unreal upsurge of the Muslims of India in the seven years following the adoption of the Lahore resolution, blinded the leaders of Muslim India and made them demand a single Pakistan comprising the two Muslim majority areas of the sub-continent. Voices were raised off and on in East Bengal regarding the interests of the Muslims of Bengal in a future Pakistan. In 1941 A. K. Fazlul Haq, who had moved the Lahore resolution, resigned from the Muslim League, alleging that the interests of the Bengali Muslims would never be safeguarded by a party which was largely meant to cater to the needs of the Muslims of the Muslim minority areas. The Secretary of the Bengal Muslim League, Abul Hashim, tried to raise the question of the relationship between the two Muslim majority areas of the sub-continent in a future Pakistan during the Muslim League Legislators' Convention in Delhi in 1946. He was hooted and heckled. In 1947 the Muslim League Chief Minister of Bengal, H. S. Suhrawardy, raised the slogan of a united, independent Bengal to escape the domination of the All-India Muslim League. These voices were, however, steam-rollered by the leaders of the Muslim League who cashed in on the communal frenzy that overtook all parts of the sub-continent, including Bengal, in the middle forties.

The unnatural relationship between East Bengal and West Pakistan was sustained in the early years of freedom by a number of factors. East Bengal was represented in the Constituent Assembly of Pakistan by the hard core of the conservative elements in the Muslim League, and among the 44 representatives of the province in the Constituent Assembly there were a number of Muslim leaders from other areas of India such as Liaquat Ali Khan, Ishtiaq Hassan Qureshi and Mahmud Hussain. In fact, the displaced Indian Muslim elite which migrated to Pakistan continued to provide the leadership to the new state for the first three years. Both Governor-General Jinnah and Prime Minister Liaquat Ali Khan were from the Muslim minority provinces of India and thus equi-distant from the demands and aspirations—political, economic and cultural—of the people of West Pakistan on the one hand and Bengal on the other. This domination of an alien elite paradoxically appeared to be resolving Pakistan's problems of unity and identity. The Indo-Muslim migrant elite succeeded in holding the two wings of Pakistan together by manipulating the Indo-Islamic consciousness created in the wake of the developments of 1946-47.

A measure of the self-confidence of the Indo-Muslim elite in Pakistan was its attempt to impose Urdu on the people of East and West Pakistan, few of whom spoke or understood the language. The unreality of the control exercised over the whole of Pakistan by an entirely alien elite became clear as the new state settled down as an autonomous political and cultural entity. The refugees from India who ruled the roost in Pakistan in its early years were equally unwelcome as rulers to the Punjabis and the Bengalis. This alien power elite in Karachi had to yield place to a new power elite composed of the sons of the soil in West Pakistan. The challenge to this structure came from the Punjab which wanted to assert its legitimate rights. As Prime Minister Liaquat Ali Khan was frantically trying to retain his control over the new state, he discovered the Rawalpindi conspiracy case in 1950. And it was in Rawalpindi, now the centre of Government in Pakistan, that he was murdered a year later.

The assassination of Liaquat Ali Khan has never been properly explained. A large section of opinion in Pakistan, particularly among the migrants from India, have always suspected the hand of high officials and top politicians in this murder, and Begum Liaquat Ali Khan has year after year been demanding a proper enquiry. But whatever might have been the cause of this murder, it is clear in retrospect that the elimination of the Indo-Muslim leadership created conditions for a confrontation between Punjab and Bengal.

The power structure which evolved in Karachi after the murder of Liaquat Ali Khan had a much larger Punjabi component than the earlier power structure. Ghulam Mohammad, a civil servant, with a long record of service to British authorities in India, became the Governor-General and laid the foundations of what is now known as the military-bureaucratic complex in Pakistan. For a time he kept the Bengal Muslim League leader, Nazimuddin, as his Prime Minister and a tenuous Bengali-Punjabi combination appeared to be ruling at the centre. By early 1953, however, Ghulam Mohammad mustered the courage to dismiss Nazimuddin though the latter still had the support of the majority in the Pakistan Constituent Assembly.

The dismissal of Nazimuddin was also brought about through conspiratorial methods. In 1952 the Chief Minister of Punjab, Mian Mumtaz Daultana, unleashed havoc in the streets of Lahore in the form of an anti-Ahmedia agitation. The small sect of Punjabi Muslims known as the Ahmedias were anathema to the mainstream of the Muslims of the province. However, it was an Ahmedia, Mohammad Zafrullah Khan, who was the most significant representative of Punjab in the Central Cabinet at that time, and the agitation against the Ahmedias was launched, among other things, to have Zafrullah Khan dismissed. The Ahmedias were also to be designated a non-Muslim minority. The law and order situation in Lahore deteriorated very sharply and martial law was reimposed.

The anti-Ahmedia agitation served two goals: for the first time the army was brought into the political life of Pakistan as a peace-enforcing machine; secondly, a conflict was created between the provincial government of Punjab and the Central Government, which was still headed by Nazimuddin. The

Central Government succeeded in dismissing Mian Mumtaz Daultana, the Chief Minister of Punjab, but soon afterwards Governor-General Ghulam Mohammad arbitrarily dismissed the Nazimuddin government also.

In his search for a pliable Bengali, Ghulam Mohammad had to go up to Washington, where Mohammed Ali Bogra was then the Ambassador. This non-descript Bengali politician was brought from the United States to head the government of Pakistan, thus further weakening the association of East Bengal with the Central Government.

Within the bureaucracy, the contest was between the refugees from India and the sons of the soil of West Pakistan. East Bengal was totally insignificant in the bureaucratic apparatus. The political happenings in Karachi had an impact on the distribution of power within the Pakistani bureaucracy and the Punjabi elite gradually eased out the refugees from positions of power and authority. One of the key bureaucrats who played an extremely important role in the evolution of the military-bureaucratic complex was General Iskander Mirza. Of dubious origin, Iskander Mirza was tipped by the British Government in India for an important role in the Political Department, particularly in controlling the ebullient Pathans of the North-West Frontier Province. Iskander Mirza provided the link between the army and the bureaucracy of Pakistan and in the structure which Ghulam Mohammad evolved he happened to be a very important person. Another key figure was General Ayub Khan, from the district of Hazara, where Punjabis and Pathans co-exist. It is now known that General Ayub Khan was taken into confidence by Ghulam Mohammad in the very early years of his rule and that it was as far back as 1954 that Ghulam Mohammad asked Ayub Khan to take over the Government of Pakistan.

As the nascent structure of the military-bureaucratic complex began to take shape, two other significant developments were occurring in Pakistan. In East Bengal the Muslim League was becoming irrelevant, as was proved in the elections held in March, 1954. The Muslim League issued an appeal to the people of East Bengal, signed by almost all the top leaders of the party, asking them to vote for the League on the ground that a vote against it would be a vote against Pakistan. In response to that appeal, the Muslims of East Bengal returned only nine Muslim Leaguers to the provincial assembly in which there were 237 Muslim seats. A united front of the Awami League and the Krishak Praja Party won 224. Thus as Punjab was taking over power at the centre, Bengal was politically preparing itself for a confrontation with it.

The second development was of even greater significance. The United States of America in particular and the West in general came down heavily on the side of the military bureaucratic complex by providing enormous military assistance to Pakistan. It is well-known that by the end of 1953 all the three key figures in the new power structure of Pakistan, Ghulam Mohammad, Iskander Mirza and Ayub Khan, were negotiating military assistance for Pakistan with Washington. The formal announcement of military aid came in March, 1954, exactly at a time when East Bengal was rejecting the Muslim League and electing the United Front as the political organisation of its choice.

It is American military aid to Pakistan and the involvement of international forces on the side of the military bureaucratic elite that tipped the balance heavily in favour of the non-Bengali elite. The Bengalis had but little influence within the army or the bureaucracy. It was only through politics that the people of East Bengal could have asserted their legitimate rights and interests. By providing military aid to Pakistan, the U.S.A. emerged as the underwriter of the military and the bureaucracy as the dominant elements in the power structure of Pakistan—a phenomenon which relegated the Bengali to a position of insignificance.

It is worthwhile to take a look at this point at the nature of the Bengali Muslim leadership which has been trying to challenge the authority of the Muslim League in East Bengal. In the history of Bengali Muslim politics, three figures stood out: Nazimuddin, Suhrawardy and Fazlul Haq. Nazimuddin, a scion of the Nawab family of Dacca, which had a lot to do with the formation of the All-India Muslim League in 1906, was a feudal aristocrat *par excellence*. He spoke no Bengali and had little knowledge or understanding of the mind of the middle-class Bengalis of either the rural or urban areas. His relationship with the Muslim League throughout his life was one of total loyalty, if not of subservience. H. S. Suhrawardy spoke little Bengali and belonged to an urban middle-class

family which produced distinguished civil servants and edu-
cationists. He had learnt his politics in the early years at the
feet of C. R. Das and was at one stage a colleague of Subhas
Chandra Bose. He had mastered the technique of managing
urban politics, including utilisation of hoodlums for political
purposes. In essence, Suhrawardy represented the aspirations
of the Muslim urban middle-classes among the Bengalis. His
relationship with the All-India Muslim League was one of
ambivalence, as was evident from the fluctuations in the level
of his relationship with Mohammed Ali Jinnah in the years
before the partition. A. K. Fazlul Haq was a Bengali from an
interior district of East Bengal with a middle peasant background. He essentially represented the urges of the Muslim
peasantry in East Bengal and a government run by him in
1937 in the province of Bengal had brought about strikingly
progressive land reforms, which compared well with those conceived by the Congress governments in other parts of India.
Fazlul Haq's relationship with the Muslim League was anta-
gonistic, except for very brief periods of his chequered career.

After the partition, while Nazimuddin went away to Karachi
to participate in the central affairs of Pakistan, Suhrawardy
and Haq combined in a united front to create a massive opposition to the Muslim League in East Bengal. It is this combination, representing at the same time the urges of the urban
and rural middle-classes among the Bengali Muslims, which
succeeded in enlisting the support of a number of younger
and more radical leaders among the Bengali Muslims, such
as Maulana Bhashani, Mujibur Rehman and Ataur Rehman. In fact, it was during the United Front's electoral struggle
against the Muslim League in 1954 that Mujibur Rehman
emerged as a front rank political leader of East Bengal.

As has been said earlier, while East Bengal was preparing
to confront West Pakistan with a combination of heterogeneous
Bengali forces, the West Pakistani elite was getting ready for
it with the help of international forces. Following the elections
in 1954, Fazlul Haq became the Chief Minister of East Bengal
and promptly visited Calcutta for discussions with the political
leaders of West Bengal in order to improve relations between
the two Bengals. The rise of this elite was anathema to the
Government in Karachi. According to the leaders of East Bengal, the Central Government engineered a riot in the city of

Narayanganj between Bengalis and non-Bengalis at this time and used it as the excuse, along with the speeches made by him during his visit to Calcutta in 1954, for charging Fazlul Haq with treason, among other things, and summarily dismissing him, just as earlier, in 1948, Suhrawardy was charged with treason and detained in Dacca. Not only was Fazlul Haq dismissed and the constitution suspended in East Bengal, but the formidable Iskander Mirza was sent as the new Governor of the province. Notice was thus served that the central authority would, if necessary, use force to suppress the people of East Bengal.

This demonstration of the strength and determination of the Centre to hold down the people of East Pakistan came after deep distrust and suspicion between the two wings had manifested itself in the Constituent Assembly of Pakistan. The Assembly, which was constituted in 1947, had not begun serious deliberations on the future constitution of Pakistan till 1951. All that had happened earlier was the passing of an Objectives Resolution, which Prime Minister Liaquat Ali Khan had moved in 1949 with the declaration that while for geographical reasons Pakistan had to be a federation, the goal was to build a single united Pakistani nation on Islamic lines.

Both the objectives proved hard to accomplish. There was little agreement among the Ulema—the religious leaders of Pakistani society—as to what Islam should mean for Pakistan and how Islamic principles should be adumbrated in the constitution. As the noted Canadian scholar on Pakistan, Wilfred Cantwell Smith, said in another context, there was in Pakistan in its early years "the sorry spectacle of Muslim divines, none of whom agreed on the definition of the Muslim, and who yet were practically unanimous that all who disagreed should be put to death". In the Basic Principles Committee of the Pakistan Constituent Assembly, the pressure of the Ulema was felt. Not only was Pakistan engaged in a search for an Islamic identity; it had delegated to an utterly reactionary theocratic group like the Ulema the task of defining the role of Islam in the fundamental law of Pakistan.

It is instructive to look back at some of the recommendations of the Basic Principles Committee regarding what were known as the Islamic features of the constitution. First, the Head of State would be a Muslim. Though nothing was said specifically about the heads of units, their oaths as laid down in the report signified that they too would be Muslims. Second, it was to be written into the body of the constitution and not only in the list of directive principles that no law could be enacted which was repugnant to the holy *Quran* and the *Sunnah*. Third, if during the discussion on any bill (excepting money bills) in any house of the legislature, any member said that the bill was repugnant to the holy *Quran* or the *Sunnah*, the Head of State, before giving his assent to it, would refer the bill to an advisory board of five Ulema which would be set up by him. If the Board unanimously recommended changes in it, or rejected it, the Head of State would send the bill back to the legislature with a message asking for consideration in the light of the recommendations of the Board. After that, the bill, in order to receive the assent of the Head of State, would have to be passed not only by a majority of the members present and voting but by a majority of the Muslim members present and voting. In case of a difference of opinion among the five members of the Board, the Head of State would act in his discretion in giving assent to the bill or withholding it. Similar functions would be constituted in the units.

Of the eighteen directive principles of state policy, the first five were to provide an Islamic direction to the government of the country. It was said for example, that the teachings of the holy *Quran* should be compulsory learning for Muslims and that *Riba* (interest) should be eliminated. It was also made clear in the B.P.C. report that Muslims would be treated as a separate political entity and there would be communal representation at all levels of government.

The retrograde character of these recommendations was obvious to almost all sections of politicians in Pakistan, most of whom were committed to the country's modernisation by one method or another. But the Ulema had come to occupy an important position in the public life of West Pakistan because of the communal frenzy of the late forties. The definition of the nature of the Pakistani state by the politicians themselves had encouraged the Ulema to believe that they constituted an important lever of power in Pakistani society. It was natural, therefore, that they should have attempted to take over the function of defining the ideology of the Pakistani state.

Paradoxically, the very attempt to define the ideology of

Pakistan and to delineate the place of Islam in society made this ideology irrelevant to the politically articulate elements in the two wings of Pakistan. Thanks to the long exposure of the two wings to western rule, old fashioned Islamic ideas were bound to appear irrelevant to the political elite. Any attempt to convert Pakistan into a theocratic state would be resisted by them just as the Ulema were bound to try to create a theocratic state in order to circumvent the processes of western democracy in Pakistani society. The resulting hiatus between those who thought of an ideology for Pakistan and those who were concerned with the more mundane problems of erecting a power structure created an impossible constitutional tussle. The problem of evolving a suitable federal structure became acute as a result of the complete insulation of the Islamic ideologues as represented by the Ulema from the practical politicians as represented by leaders of the Muslim League in the various provinces. The latter naturally became unconcerned about larger issues of the political philosophy of Pakistan and concentrated their energies on devising a federal structure.

The problem of federalism in Pakistan was dual. A structure had to be evolved for West Pakistan where Sind, N.W.F.P. and Baluchistan were zealous of their separate rights and were disinclined to accept the domination of Punjab. Much more important, however, was the growing East-West schism which was accentuated by the meaningless controversy over Islam and by the elimination of the "Indian" component in the Pakistani leadership. In the early phases, the attitude of the elite of West Pakistan towards East Pakistan was so hard that they could not even agree to the acceptance of Bengali as one of the national languages of Pakistan. In the Basic Principles Committee report, Urdu was recommended as *the* national lauguage. There was violent reaction to this in East Bengal where all sections were united behind the demand for making Bengali a national language. More than a dozen lives were lost in Dacca in February, 1952, when a violent agitation for Bengali broke out in the city. The elite in West Pakistan was, however, convinced that Bengali, with a script based on Devanagri and with a Sanskrit vocabulary, smacked too much of Hindu culture and had to be given up in favour of Urdu, which was more "Islamic" in origin. They also used the additional argument that it was the will of the founder of Pakistan, M. A.

Jinnah, that Urdu should be the only national language!

Feelings in East Pakistan were, however, strong on the issue and even under the leadership of the Muslim League the provincial assembly had to pass a unanimous resolution demanding that Bengali be made a national language. In fact the demand for Bengali became the focal point of an emerging national identity in East Bengal. Feelings ran so high on this issue that in early 1953 an All-Pakistan History Conference which was to run for three days had to be declared ended on the second because the president of the Conference had made some unkind remarks about Bengali in his inaugural address.

The Constituent Assembly of Pakistan came up against formidable problems in defining the place of various provinces of Pakistan in the federal structure. Opinions in the two wings of Pakistan on this subject were so diverse that the Muslim League leaders found it impossible to bring about a compromise formula. All that they achieved was to have the principle of parity of representation between East and West Pakistan accepted. This was in contravention of the principle of representation according to population and some sections of East Bengali opinion resented the idea of parity. But the more important problem was that while parity was accepted in principle, the actual delineation of the representation in terms of the two houses of the central legislature proved to be an intractable problem.

It is interesting to recall that even at this stage some sections of left-wing opinion in Pakistan, particularly in Punjab, had foreseen that only a confederation between the two zones of Pakistan would suit the peculiar geographical realities of the country. As the *Pakistan Times* wrote in an editorial on December 30, 1952, "the vast difference between East and West Pakistan, the language question, the difference in the cultural outlook of the people of the two wings and the diverse nature of their economic problems render a centralised form of government unfeasible". The newspaper, which was then pronouncedly leftist in its views, also drew attention to that part of the Lahore resolution which wanted autonomous and sovereign independent states to be set up in the two Muslim majority areas of the Indian sub-continent.

The confederal idea had the support of two progressive Muslim Leaguers of Punjab, Mian Iftikharuddin and Shaukat

29

Hayat Khan, and ofcourse, of the leaders of the East Bengal Awami League and the East Bengal Congress. The substance of the confederal demand was incorporated in an amendment jointly tabled by two Congress members of the Pakistan Constituent Assembly, J. C. Majumdar and D. N. Dutta (who is reported to have been brutally killed last April by the Pakistani army in Comilla). The idea was violently opposed by the leaders of the Muslim League, who contended that confederation would mean the end of Pakistan, as it was bound to lead to the country's ultimate division and destruction.

The plight of the Congress and the Azad Pakistan Party who saw the need for a confederation was symptomatic of the decay in the country's party political structure. Both were slandered as anti-Pakistani by the Muslim League, as indeed were all others who dared differ from the League on the undefined fundamentals of Pakistani ideology. It appears in retrospect that the strain on the unity of Pakistan was at least partly due to the fact that no political party which could develop an all-Pakistan base was allowed to function. The left-wing parties were destroyed in 1951. The Awami League, which claimed to have branches all over the country, was unable to evolve an all-Pakistan personality because of the inherent contradictions between the political mind of the two wings. Parties like the Jamaat-e-Islami had a strong base in West Pakistan but very little hold over East Bengal. Like the Congress in India, the Muslim League alone could claim to be a party with some following in all parts of the country. By 1954, however, the Muslim League was eliminated in East Bengal and soon afterwards it declined very rapidly in West Pakistan as well.

This collapse of all-Pakistan politics and the emergence of two autonomous political systems added to the difficulties of resolving problems between the two wings. Even within the Muslim League there were grave contradictions between the representatives of Bengal and those of other Pakistani provinces; outside the League there was not even a facade of unity.

The collapse of all-Pakistan politics only helped to strengthen the authority of the nascent military-bureaucratic complex. In October, 1954, Governor-General Ghulam Mohammad took the unprecedented step of dismissing the Constituent Assembly and of appointing a government of his own choice consisting of such heterogeneous elements as Iskander Mirza, Ayub Khan,

Dr. Khan Sahib and Mohammed Ali Bogra. The erosion of the authority of the political leaders, however, created grave complications for the stability of Pakistani politics. Government after government was formed in Karachi, to be dissolved or dismissed by the Governor-General. Between 1954 and 1958 Pakistan had as many as five Prime Ministers.

This phase of grave political instability paved the ground for the adoption of a constitution in 1956. The first constitution was based on the principle of parity between East and West Pakistan—a concession which leaders like Suhrawardy and Fazlul Haq found difficult to resist in the light of the fact that the United Front which had come into being in East Pakistan in 1954 had already been disrupted and atomized. Suhrawardy, who was picked up as the instrument to draft an agreed constitutional formula, made another vital concession to Punjab: he accepted the one-unit scheme. The whole of West Pakistan was integrated into a single province ruled from Lahore. The urges and aspirations of the smaller nationalities of West Pakistan could not stand in the way of this major structural change in favour of Punjab for the simple reason that these nationalities could not assert themselves without the help of the political forces of East Bengal.

In return for these two major concessions, Suhrawardy extracted from the West Pakistan elite one significant concession in regard to East Bengal, the importance of which is now more clear than it was before. He successfully insisted on the introduction of a system of joint electorates in East Bengal, whereas in West Pakistan the minorities were still to elect their own representatives to the assembly. The introduction of joint electorate was opposed by right-wing parties like the Muslim League, but the idea enjoyed the support of the vast masses of the Hindus and the Muslims of East Bengal.

This rejection of the old two-nation theory paved the ground for the evolution of a new two-nation theory. It was not Hindus and Muslims who constituted two nations in the new theory as they did in the old but Bengalis and West Pakistanis. The determination of the Muslims of East Bengal to have a system of joint electorate marked the end of the process of the discovery by them that only by denying the old two-nation theory could East Bengal assert its rights in Pakistan. The safety and security of the Hindu population in East Bengal and the evolution of a common secular nationality in the province was regarded by the Muslim elite of the area as a pre-condition for its success in undoing the stranglehold of an utterly reactionary elite over the Central Government of Pakistan.

Adoption of the Constitution did not resolve the problems of erecting a viable political structure in Pakistan. In the absence of all-Pakistan politics, the differences between the two wings became more and more acute. What is more, the politics of contrivance which led to the adoption of the Constitution only accentuated the people's misgivings about the political system and political leaders. Caught between the pressures exerted by the army and the bureaucracy on the one hand and the pressures exerted from below by the people on the other, the politicians of Pakistan lost their grip over the situation and began to function as petty men interested in the promotion of personal and factional interests rather than any larger cause. The disintegration of political life in Pakistan ultimately led to the military coup in October, 1958.

The elimination of party politics and the imposition of military rule totally destroyed the hopes of East Bengal. Its interests could not be safeguarded in a highly centralised structure for the whole of Pakistan. For the Bengalis, the meaning of the military coup was that it marked the culmination of the ascendency of the military-bureaucratic elite in Pakistan and the relegation of the leaders of political parties to a status of insignificance in public life.

The system that Ayub Khan built was not only authoritarian in character but also heavily weighted in favour of Punjab. One of the first acts of General Ayub Khan was to shift the capital from Karachi to Islamabad, which was symbolic of the decline of the refugees from India as a political force in Pakistan. It has been suggested by some that even his selective measures against corrupt civil servants tilted the balance within the civil service decisively in favour of the Punjabi elements.

For East Bengal the effects of the change in Karachi were highly adverse. In 1962 Ayub Khan gave a constitution to his country, but this meant little change in the nature of the power structure. The essential features of the structure were the rejection of the elementary principles of parliamentary democracy, the creation of a pseudo-democratic state with the help of the so-called basic democracies, and the protection and perpetuation of the military-bureaucratic complex as the source of power and authority.

From the viewpoint of East Bengal, a power structure in which the army, the civil service and the politicians constituted the three props of the power tripod was utterly irrelevant. For one thing, the political leg was bound to be less important than the other two in such a system. President Ayub viewed the function of political parties as all authoritarian leaders have done—as an instrument of public relations for a government the source of whose authority lies outside the party system. The way he created a Muslim League of his own in Pakistan was symptomatic of his approach to the role of a political party.

For East Bengal the problem was that party politics, which was the only means available to it for asserting its rights within Pakistan, had now become insignificant. In neither the army nor the bureaucracy was East Pakistan a major factor. At the end of a decade of Ayub's benevolent dictatorship East Pakistan's share in the armed forces was less than 10%; it was not much higher in the top ranks of the civil service. The three-leg structure of power and authority in Pakistan was thus totally irrelevant for the people of East Bengal.

What was equally important was the philosophy and outlook of the dictatorship in Pakistan. President Ayub Khan chose to publish his autobiography in 1967 and the document revealed a fantastic degree of suspicion, distrust and contempt for the East Bengali in the mind of the country's President. It is worthwhile to quote a few extracts from President Ayub Khan's writings to illustrate his views on East Bengal.

In the chapter entitled "Constitution and Ideology", Ayub Khan reproduced the text of a document prepared in 1954 on the contemporary and future problems of Pakistan. That document had the following to say on the mind of the East Bengali:

> *The people of Pakistan consist of a variety of races, each with its own historical background and culture. East Bengalis, who constitute the bulk of the population, probably belong to the very original Indian races. It would be no exaggeration to say that up to the creation of Pakis-*

*tan, they had not known any real freedom or sove-
reignty. They have been in turn ruled either by the caste
Hindus, Moghuls, Pathans, or the British. In addition,
they have been and still are under considerable Hindu
cultural and linguistic influence. As such they have all
the inhibitions of down-trodden races and have not yet
found it possible to adjust psychologically to the requirements of the new-born freedom. Their popular complexes,
exclusiveness, suspicion and a sort of defensive aggres-
siveness probably emerge from this historical background.*[1]

In the same chapter, the President of Pakistan implied that
the disparity between West Pakistan and East Pakistan was
largely a result of the difference in the capacity of the two
peoples:

*... I must refer to a phenomenon which has been the cause
of considerable tension and misunderstanding between the
two Provinces. This is the slogan of 'disparity', which
has assumed considerable social significance and usually
refers to an assumed lack of equality between the two
provinces of the country. It is a much-abused word and
covers a wide variety of complaints and grievances, very
often of a personal character. If a candidate does not
have the requisite qualifications and is, therefore, not
selected for a job, he dubs it 'disparity' ...
Now disparity is recognised by all and so is the need to
remove disparity. What is not realised is that 'disparity'
is a phase in the process of development...
It is inconceivable that any government should be able to
compel people in one region to work at less than their
capacity till others build up an equal capacity. It should
be the aim of a welfare State to narrow down the gaps
and eliminate imbalance, but the only way to do it is by
providing greater incentives to the relatively developed
ones. It would be a futile and self-defeating policy to
bring about uniformity by lowering levels of progress
all round.*[2]

1. *Friends Not Masters: A Political Autobiography,* Mohammad Ayub
Khan, Oxford University Press, Karachi, 1967, p. 275.
2. *Ibid.*

The President had spent a part of his life in Dacca in the early years of Pakistan as the General Officer Commanding of East Pakistan. During those days, very few Bengalis were recruited to the army and the explanation for this was given by Ayub Khan as follows:

> The thing that surprised me was the lack of manpower with qualities of leadership. The Army Selection Board would visit East Pakistan every six months. In the beginning, for the first one or two terms, the Board found four or five boys who could be accepted for the Army Military College. But they were mainly boys who had come from refugee families. When this material was exhausted they came to selection from amongst the local boys. The Selection Board would then be lucky to get even one or two borderline cases. I would advise the Board to take them anyway because nobody would accept that the Board had been fair and objective and that the rules and specifications had been rigidly applied.[3]

Also revealing was the manner in which Ayub thought he was managing the politicians of East Pakistan as early as 1948. Here are two interesting extracts from his autobiography:

> ...Fazlul Haq came out along with Mohammad Ali of Bogra, who was then in the Opposition, and they tried to work up the boys again. I tapped Mohammad Ali on the shoulder and said, 'Are you looking for a bullet?' He retorted, 'You are being rude.' I did not want the trouble to restart; so I told him firmly to go home.
>
> ...I remember one day I was coming back to the High Court after an inspection. I found Fazlul Haq asking the students to lie flat on the ground to prevent the working of the Court. I looked out of my car and asked what it was all about. Fazlul Haq saw me and apparently decided that I looked dangerous. He quietly advised the boys to clear out. I must say life was not without its moments of excitement, and even amusement, in those days.[4]

3. *Ibid.*
4. *Ibid.*

It was repeatedly claimed on behalf of Ayub Khan that during his regime important steps were taken to redress the imbalance between East and West Pakistan. It is true that till the suicidal war of 1965 the Ayub regime had succeeded in registering notable economic progress in Pakistan and at least part of the benefits of this would have flowed to the people of East Bengal. It is perhaps also true that some calculated steps were taken by his government to increase the flow of aid and investment in East Bengal and to improve the position of the East Bengali within the army and the civil service of Pakistan. These measures were, however, totally inadequate from the viewpoint of East Bengal. Much of the propaganda of the Ayub government regarding its contribution to East Bengal appeared to the East Bengali to be but an imperial white paper cleverly mustering convenient facts and figures to prove that the colonial rule had not been entirely retrograde for the subject peoples.

The sense of powerlessness of East Bengal was only accentuated by the efforts of President Ayub Khan to associate a few East Pakistanis of his choice with the task of government. Retired civil servants and police officials from East Bengal, who represented to the politically vocal and articulate East Bengalis the negation of the urges and aspirations of the people in that wing, were carefully selected to become Governors and Ministers, again in much the same way as a colonial regime tries to 'associate' a dependent people with the task of government.

It is also important to note that much of the economic progress of Pakistan during the Ayub regime was the result of the pursuit of economic policies which were calculated to help the unbridled private sector without any regard for social justice. Ambassador Aziz Ahmed proudly declared at the Far East American Council of Commerce and Industry in 1961: "Indeed by underscoring the reliance on private initiative and sensible fiscal policies, Pakistan has literally become the largest showcase of private enterprise in the under-developed Afro-Asian world. This is in sharp contrast to the discouragement of private enterprise elsewhere in the region by government controls and doctrinaire philosophies."

Towards the end of the Ayub regime, glaring inequalities in the economy of Pakistan were revealed. Almost the entire benefit of industrial development had been confined to about 20 families of Pakistan. What was more interesting was the nature of the industrial elite that was encouraged to expand and the methods through which they did so. It was quite obvious that the new industrial class of Pakistan was sharing its profits with the military-bureaucratic complex through institutionalised corruption of various sorts. The Muslim industrial elite of British India, like the house of the Ispahanis, was relegated to a position of relative insignificance because of its inability to pursue the new practices, whereas entirely unknown families who were not engaged in industrial activity in pre-partition times, emerged as major corporations.

In the field of land reforms also, the measures taken under President Ayub Khan were calculated to stabilise the upper peasantry of the Punjab while demolishing the jagirdars of Sind, Bhawalpur and Baluchistan. The Punjabi landed aristocracy was virtually unhurt by the land reforms of July, 1959, which imposed a ceiling on ownership at 500 acres of irrigated land and 1,000 acres of non-irrigated land.

The military-bureaucratic complex of Pakistan was providing the political infrastructure needed for the exploitation of the people of Pakistan by the industrial and feudal elite. Its own gains in the process could be well illustrated by the fact that the son of President Ayub Khan emerged as a major operator on the industrial scene during his father's regime.

Inequitable and oppressive as this economic structure was for the whole of Pakistan, it was particularly so for the people of East Bengal. There was hardly any indigenous Bengali enterprise in East Bengal, all major industries being in the hands of the same families which dominated West Pakistan. Employment and other opportunities opened up by the expansion of private enterprise were largely taken advantage of by the middle-classes of West Pakistan. The hopes of the people of East Bengal, like the hopes of under-privileged people anywhere, lay in the expansion of the public sector and in the management of that sector by a democratically elected government.

The political, economic and social implications of a military dictatorship in Islamabad were thus utterly retrograde from the viewpoint of East Bengal. The war of 1965, which imposed heavy burdens on the people of Pakistan but was unleashed in the interests of the elite of West Pakistan, came as the proverbial last straw on the back of the East Bengal camel. It exposed to the people of East Bengal some hidden aspects of West Pakistani colonialism. East Pakistan was left entirely without any defence when the war broke out, just as the Asian colonies of West European powers were left defenceless in 1941. Having paid through its nose for the ever-escalating military budget of Pakistan, the East Bengalis discovered that the benefits of the war preparations were concentrated entirely in the western wing.

They also became convinced that the whole structure of Pakistan's foreign relations, based on the principle of continued hostility towards India, was one of the methods through which the elite in West Pakistan was trying to retain its stranglehold over East Pakistan. The rift between East Bengal and the rulers of Pakistan grew as a result of the 1965 war, and the schism that had been developing in Pakistan since 1947 now became irreparable.

The utterly insecure regime tried various methods of subjugating the people of East Bengal and was finally driven to launch the so-called 'Agartala conspiracy case' against Mujibur Rehman and other leaders of East Bengal. Instead of diverting the attention of the people of East Bengal from their struggle against West Pakistan, the case proved to be a traumatic experience for the people of East Bengal who had now been provided with a most vivid glimpse of the callous and cynical attitude of the military dictatorship towards them.

The country-wide agitation which swept the Ayub regime off its feet and brought General Yahya Khan into power provided East Pakistan with a measure of hope that its national aspirations could be achieved through peaceful agitation. Shortly before he was forced to give up office, Ayub Khan himself admitted that fundamental changes were needed in Pakistan if the country was to continue as a single entity. He said in his broadcast of February 21, 1969: "I am fully conscious of the dissatisfaction that exists in the country with the present system of elections. People want direct elections on the basis of adult franchise. I realise also that the intelligentsia feels left out and wants a greater say in the affairs of the state. People of East Pakistan believe that in the present system they are not equal partners and also they do not have full control over the affairs of the province. There is also the feeling that the National and Provincial Assemblies do not possess the powers which they are entitled to have under a democratic system."

As Yahya Khan came to power in March, 1969, the question that bothered the people of East Bengal was whether the history of Pakistan had come full circle with the imposition of another martial law, and whether the old regime would continue under "Tweedle Khan" (as a well-known British weekly put it) or the new dictator was sincere in saying that he was preparing the conditions for an early and smooth transfer of power to the representatives of the people elected freely and impartially on the basis of adult franchise.

Recent events have belied the hopes of the optimists and confirmed the fears of the pessimists. East Bengal's struggle against a primitive colonial rule has ceased to be a constitutional struggle and the people of Bangla Desh have proclaimed their independence. However long and protracted the struggle, it is inconceivable that the determination and will of 75 million Bengalis to regain their freedom will ever be suppressed. The story of the rise and fall of Pakistan is a story of the lack of viability of an artificial nationalism based on religion, a story of military-bureaucratic oligarchy; it is a story of lack of moral authority, and of the inability of a political system to sustain itself when it does not cater to the economic and social needs of a deprived population.

The rise of the freedom movement in Bangla Desh has also thrown up certain issues which are of wider relevance—issues of internal colonisation in some of the new states—which have been overlooked by a *status quo* oriented international system in its desire to preserve a tenuous system of states in the world. If the strains created by geographical absurdity were by themselves unique and formidable, they were only accentuated by the attempt to build up an authoritarian political infrastructure to preserve an unjust social system in West Pakistan and a colonial relationship between the two wings of what was once known as Pakistan. The atrocities suffered by the people of Bangla Desh should help to wake up the world to these issues.

FROM MARTIAL LAW TO
BANGLA DESH

MOHAMMED AYOOB

WHETHER BY accident or design, President Yahya Khan selected
the second anniversary of his accession to power as the date
for unleashing the unprecedented wave of repression and terror
on the people of East Bengal. The fateful night of March 25-26
saw the concept of Pakistan buried under the bodies of those
who were so mercilessly mowed down by the West Pakistani
army. Superficially speaking, the events of that night were an
anti-climax to the process which had started with the overthrow
of President Ayub Khan and the assumption of office by President Yahya Khan on March 25, 1969. But in a much more
significant sense the suppression of East Bengali aspirations was
the culmination of a trend which had always been operative
in Pakistani politics, whether under Ghulam Mohammad,
Iskander Mirza, Ayub Khan or Yahya Khan.

The entire political structure of Pakistan, with or without
the veneer of parliamentary democracy, was built upon three
fundamental assumptions: the supremacy of the permanent
executive over representative institutions, the dominance of
West Pakistan, especially Punjab, over East Bengal, and the
financial autonomy of the army, which meant in real terms

a very high level of expenditure (approximately, 55 per cent of the annual revenue budget) on the upkeep of the armed forces. While such a high level of defence expenditure was justified in terms of a presumed Indian threat, it had in actual fact become an end in itself; with the top echelons dominated by West Pakistanis, the defence expenditure became an aspect of western domination over the eastern wing.

If any of the three fundamental assumptions were threatened, the ruling elite was bound to react violently though the degree of violence might depend upon the magnitude of the threat and the source from which it came. As it turned out the Awami League's phenomenal victory in the first-ever general elections held in the country threatened all the three assumptions as they had never been threatened before. This explains the barbaric violence of the reaction that followed.

The events of 1969-71 cannot be fully comprehended unless they are studied within this framework and in relation to what had happened immediately before General Yahya Khan's assumption of power in March, 1969. The movement which forced the resignation of President Ayub was not a single monolith. In fact, there were two movements interrelated to, and interacting with, each other which in conjunction brought about his downfall. First, there was the movement for political freedoms which, during the last days of President Ayub's rule, assumed almost revolutionary proportions. This movement, at least in its last phase, began in West Pakistan but reached its culmination when the urban intelligentsia of East Pakistan, after overcoming their initial scepticism about West Pakistan's political stamina, joined in to wrest adult franchise and parliamentary democracy from the unwilling hands of the Field Marshal. The other was the distinct yet interrelated movement for provincial autonomy in East Bengal which had struck deep roots in the Bengali soil. This movement, while it was an exclusively East Pakistani phenomenon, found invaluable support and sustenance from the country-wide anti-Ayub agitation for political freedoms.

It would have been difficult if not impossible for the agitation for political freedoms in Pakistan to achieve the near success that it did without the simmering socio-economic as well as political discontent in East Pakistan. Similarly, it would have been extremely difficult for the autonomy movement in East Bengal to reach the tremendous proportions it did at that stage without the pitch having been first prepared by the countrywide and intense agitation for political reforms.

The ruling elite of Pakistan had, therefore, to respond to two interrelated and interacting movements rather than a single monolith. In the initial stages an effort was made to contain both the movements. It was soon realised, however, that taking into consideration the political climate in the country, this would be impossible.

The second stage of the establishment's response took the shape of President Ayub's policy of "graduated retreat" in the face of the demand for political freedoms. Hence the grant of adult franchise and the restoration of parliamentary democracy. This was considered adequate to appease, by and large, West Pakistani opposition leaders and a section of the "moderates" in East Pakistan. As for the movement for East Pakistani autonomy, the decision was taken to stand firm and, if the worst came to the worst, impose Martial Law.

This was the order of events during the last days of the Ayub regime. The Round Table Conference of March, 1969, was used as a platform to announce the grant of adult franchise and a return to the parliamentary system. The West Pakistani leadership had every reason to be pleased both with itself and with Ayub. Although Sheikh Mujibur Rehman, Nurul Amin and S. M. Murshed from East Pakistan rejected the decision taken at the RTC, and Maulana Bhashani, the second most important leader of East Pakistan after Mujib, boycotted the meeting after calling it a hoax, and although from the western wing Bhutto did not participate, the conference succeeded in causing a split in the opposition.

After the RTC, Sheikh Mujib, who had been released from prison on February 22, 1969, specifically to take part in the conference, announced that the Democratic Action Committee (DAC)—the united front of the opposition leaders from both wings—was as dead as the dodo because West Pakistani leaders had betrayed East Bengali interests. In simple terms it meant that West Pakistani leaders, satisfied with parliamentary democracy based on adult franchise, had refused to support East Pakistan's twin demands for autonomy and representation in the National Assembly on the basis of population. Since these demands hurt the interests of West Pakistani opposition as well as the West Pakistani establishment, these opposition leaders were understandably less than enthusiastic in their support for them. It was decided at the RTC that the question of autonomy should be left to the proposed National Assembly which was to be elected on the basis of inter-wing parity.

But while the regime was able to divide the opposition as a result of this strategy, it immediately touched off a storm of protest in East Pakistan. As a result of the anti-Ayub uprising, the situation in East Pakistan was far from normal, and the failure of the RTC to meet East Pakistan's demands gave strength to those forces which had ridiculed the conference as an exercise in futility. At one stage it even seemed likely that the leadership of the movement may pass out of the hands of the Awami League into the hands of the extremists, then lumped together under the umbrella of the Bhashani-led National Awami Party. It was this fact that was partly responsible for Sheikh Mujib's denunciation of the DAC and the RTC immediately after the conference ended. In addition to being a genuine expression of East Bengali sentiments, Sheikh Mujib's stand after the RTC was also a good tactical move to keep the leadership of the autonomy movement securely in the hands of the Awami League inspite of the fact that it had participated in the Conference.

Reports of deterioration in the law and order situation in East Bengal—partly genuine and partly fabricated by the government controlled mass-media—following the failure of the RTC were grasped by the establishment as an excuse for declaring Martial Law in the country and for demonstrating to the East Pakistanis that their demand for complete autonomy would be met, if necessary, by brute physical force.

As a part of the strategy followed during the Ayub regime, President Yahya Khan, immediately on assumption of power, declared that he had no intention of going back upon the concessions made by the former President on the questions of adult franchise and parliamentary government. He also stated that he had "no ambition other than the creation of conditions conducive to the establishment of a constitutional government". As a further step towards winning over West Pakistan, President Yahya Khan declared in his broadcast of November 28, 1969, that the one-unit scheme was being scrapped. This was done in order to take the wind out of the autonomists' sails in Sind, NWFP and Baluchistan, and in order to deprive East Bengal and the Awami League of potential allies in a future political set-up in Pakistan.

That this gamble paid off became very clear with the complete rout of the Sind autonomists and the not very happy showing of the Pathan autonomists in the elections of 1970. President Yahya Khan's strategy paid handsome dividends when the actual showdown between Islamabad and Dacca became inevitable. With this source of discontent removed, at least the NWFP and Sind became further integrated into the West Pakistani system. While Baluchistan may have remained a question mark, its importance in Pakistani politics (because of its sparse and scattered population, its low level of politicisation and its small representation in the National Assembly) has remained and will continue to be marginal.

Thus the process of East Pakistan's isolation got well under way. At the same time, however, President Yahya Khan realized that unless some gestures were made to East Bengal on its two major demands of proportionate representation and provincial autonomy, it would be very difficult to prevent an immediate political explosion in that part of the country. Therefore, while announcing his intention to hold nation-wide elections President Yahya Khan also announced his decision to accord the eastern wing representation in the national legislature proportionate to its population. This, according to the Census of 1961, meant approximately 54 per cent. Having conceded the demand for one-man-one-vote, the President went on to declare that the question of autonomy (or rather the extent of autonomy) would be decided by the elected Constituent-cum-National Assembly.

These concessions to East Bengali sentiments were made apparently under the impression that no East Bengali party, including the Awami League, would be able to receive such overwhelming support in East Pakistan as to muster an absolute majority in the National Assembly, and a coalition with certain West Pakistani forces would be inevitable for it. This calculation was made on the basis of the well-known antipathy between the Awami League and the National Awami Party, led by Maulana Bhashani—the second most important group in East Bengal—which seemed to preclude any major post-electoral understanding among East Bengali politicians.

Over and above all this were the powers reserved to himself

by the President under the Legal Framework Order of March 30, 1970, under which the elections were to be held. Under the LFO any constitutional document approved by the future Constituent Assembly was to come into force only when authenticated by the President, and the National Assembly was to be dissolved if the President refused such authentication. Thus, President Yahya Khan, representing the interests of the army and the West Pakistani establishment, was accorded the status of the supreme arbiter of the nation's constitutional future.

It is interesting to note that it was Maulana Bhashani who was the first categorically to denounce the President's post-ponement of a decision on the autonomy issue. According to the NAP leader, just as President Yahya Khan had dissolved the one unit in West Pakistan prior to the elections, he should have also issued an order granting provincial autonomy to East Pakistan so as to remove the issue altogether from the electoral arena. At one stage Maulana Bhashani and his NAP also threatened to boycott the elections unless the demand for provincial autonomy was granted before the elections were held.

On the other hand the Awami League did not object to a decision on autonomy being shelved for the time being, and it was probably the only East Bengal party not to denounce the postponement. The reasons for this stance were obvious. The autonomy plank was not only the election platform of the Awami League but had become its very *raison d'etre*. With this issue decided one way or the other, the League's hold on the electorate would have declined seriously. If President Yahya Khan had accepted the demand, whether on the basis of the Awami League's six-point programme or some formula which came quite close to it, the Awami League's electoral prospects might have been seriously threatened since the main plank of the party would have become irrelevant. On the other hand, if the regime's response had been less than satisfactory from the Bengali point of view, the League might have found itself faced with a protest movement, which had every likeli-hood of turning violent and opening up two dangers: one the leadership of the movement passing into the hands of more extremist elements; and two, the elections receding into the background and with them the chances of the Awami League coming to power in East Bengal.

Therefore, at this stage the Awami League's interests seemed to converge with those of the army-bureaucracy establishment. Both were interested in postponing a decision on the question of autonomy for their own reasons. The Awami League wanted to ride to electoral victory on its autonomy plank and the regime wanted to defuse the situation by putting the onus of a decision regarding autonomy on a future political set-up where East Bengal would be forced to compromise and whittle down its demands under the pressure of coalition politics.

For a variety of reasons these assumptions turned out to be out of tune with the reality. The outcome of the elections confounded both the advisers of Yahya Khan as well as the supporters of the Awami League. The elections in East Bengal turned out to be a referendum on the Awami League's six-point charter of autonomy rather than a voters' choice between viable political alternatives. There were a number of reasons which cumulatively produced such a result. First, of course, was the sense of accumulated resentment harboured by the Bengali middle-class which had also percolated down to other strata of East Bengal society. This resentment was born out of a deep-seated feeling of political ineffectiveness and economic stagnation which no one seems to have been able to gauge fully.

Another reason could have been the withdrawal of the left forces from the electoral arena. Both the NAPs—one led by Professor Muzaffar Ahmed and the other by Maulana Bhashani —decided to boycott the elections almost at the eleventh hour when the regime refused to accede to their demand for a postponement of the elections following the unprecedented natural calamity which befell the coastal districts of East Bengal on November 12, 1970. To a close observer of the East Bengal scene it was evident that both these parties were using the tidal wave as an excuse to withdraw from an electoral battle in which they had hardly any chances of putting up a good show.

The so-called pro-Moscow section of the NAP, after the split of the parent body in late 1967, had been very much on the fringe of the left movement in East Pakistan. In fact, by 1970 it has become indistinguishable from the Awami League in the eyes of the common people. This had tended to make it redundant in East Bengal's politics. Muzaffar Ahmed, in fact, tried his best to enter into an electoral alliance with the

Awami League but his offer was spurned by the Awami League leadership.

What was known as the pro-Peking wing of the NAP, led by Maulana Bhashani though dominated by committed Marxists on the organizational side, was not exclusively a communist party. It was an umbrella under which various shades of leftists, from social democrats to Maoists, had found shelter. Tariq Ali's description of Maulana Bhashani as a "non-theoretical, semi-religious believer in the peasant revolution" fits him best. His charismatic hold on the peasants of East Pakistan, especially in northern, north-central and north-eastern Bengal, was and continues to be great. At one stage, after political activity was resumed in Pakistan in 1969-70, it was expected that the Bhashani-led NAP would pose a serious challenge to the Awami League and would emerge as the second largest party in East Bengal. However, as it turned out, the NAP's challenge to the Awami League fizzled out quite a few months before the elections.

A large section of the organized left led by Mohammed Toaha, General Secretary of the East Pakistan NAP, (possibly the Nagi Reddy of East Bengal) and Abdul Huq, leader of the peasant wing of the NAP, left the party on the question of participation in the forthcoming elections. They argued that such participation would not serve the ends of a socialist revolution and would only give respectability to bourgeois democracy. With this split the NAP became organizationally very weak. Moreover, even in the rump NAP a continuous struggle went on between the Pabna group led by Abdul Matin and Allauddin (who had ideological affinities with Charu Mazumdar) and the relatively moderate and non-Marxist group led by the treasurer of the party, Anwar Zahid, who had been expelled some years ago from the underground Communist Party of East Pakistan for anti-party activities.

As a result of the defections and the in-fighting among various factions, the NAP was unable to present itself as a viable socialist alternative to the Awami League. In fact, it could put up only 15 candidates for East Pakistan's 162 elected seats in the National Assembly. On the eve of the elections Maulana Bhashani decided to boycott them and not a single NAP (Bhashani) candidate was returned either to the National or Provincial Assemblies.

47

Another factor that contributed to the Awami League's landslide victory was the natural calamity, unprecedent even for East Pakistan, which befell the coastal districts in November, 1970. The charge of callousness levelled against the West Pakistan-dominated centre by the East Bengal leaders after the cyclone, which was to a certain extent, substantiated by foreign observers, added to East Bengal's resolve to give an overwhelming mandate to the Awami League as the spokesman of East Bengal's interests. All these events led logically to the Awami League's phenomenal victory in the election of December, 1970.

The significance of the victory in terms of the future was related to the character of the Awami League. The League began immediately after the partition, as the revolt of East Bengal's infant but growing middle-class against the rule of the well-entrenched alliance of the top echelons of the army, the bureaucracy and monopoly capital based in West Pakistan. The political leadership of West Pakistan, primarily drawn from the feudal aristocracy of the Punjab and the refugee elite from Karachi, closely cooperated with this ruling alliance. The Dacca based leaders of the Awami League were successful in establishing rapport with middle peasantry of East Bengal because they themselves belonged to the recently urbanised section of this strata. Because of the low level as well as the recent origins of urbanisation in East Bengal, the city dwelling middle-class—professionals, intellectuals and white-collar workers—had intimate contacts and strong family ties with the Bengali countryside. Thus they were able to draw the more politicized sections of the rural population also into their struggle for a place in the sun.

As the emphasis of the movement shifted from language and culture to economics and politics the Awami League was able to project itself more and more as the foremost and, in the last stages, the exclusive spokesman of Bengali interests. As the Bengali upsurge became a national movement, the Awami League became a nationalist organisation on the lines of the pre-independence Indian National Congress. From this character of the party also flowed certain weaknesses which became very clear during the closing days of the Yahya-Mujib parleys of March, 1971. An open, amorphous organisation with a middle-class, city-based leadership, while eminently suited for fighting and winning elections and even leading a civil disobedience movement, was not the sort of organisation that could either prepare contingency plans for an armed resistance or hope to lead a resistance which was bound to turn into a guerrilla war.

The elections of 1970 in East Bengal, as stated earlier, virtually became a referendum on the Awami League's six-point charter of autonomy. With the leftist parties having opted out of electoral politics there was hardly any popular force left which could vie with the Awami League in electoral popularity. The three factions of the Muslim League as well as Nurul Amin's Pakistan Democratic Party were linked in the popular mind to the oppressive and exploitative Ayub regime and were, therefore, considered to be the stooges of Islamabad. The Jamat-i-Islami also suffered the same disadvantage since its religious fundamentalism militated against East Bengal's growing secular nationalism.

The Awami League's victory at the polls was total. It captured all but two of the eastern wing seats in the National Assembly and polled 72.6 per cent of the votes cast in East Bengal. It also captured all but a dozen seats in the Provincial Assembly. In the process, the Awami League won an absolute majority of seats (over 53 per cent) in Pakistan's Constituent-cum-National Assembly. It was this absolute majority which, more than anything else, triggered off the constitutional crisis in Pakistan.

The extent of the Awami League's victory had not been anticipated by the regime in Islamabad. Nor by the League itself. While it had been generally expected that the League would secure a large majority of the East Bengal seats no one anticipated the clean sweep that it made. Had the Awami League been able to secure about 115 to 120 seats, as anticipated by Islamabad, it would still have been far short of a majority in the National Assembly. This would have forced the League to make compromises in order to gain the support of certain West Pakistani elements to frame the Constitution and form the central government. Even more important, the League would then have been able to justify any compromises made by it to its own constituency in East Bengal without committing political harakiri.

The election results upset all these calculations. The massive mandate the Awami League received converted its six-point programme into the minimum, non-negotiable demands of East Bengal, and the League, now reflecting the mood of the entire province, became the prisoner of its own victory. Pressures began to mount both from within and outside the party that the six-point programme must be considered sacrosanct and implemented in full; any compromise would be now considered a betrayal of Bangla Desh. Not only this, the demand was raised by many people, Maulana Bhashani being the foremost among them, that after its massive electoral victory, the Awami League should immediately declare the independence of Bangla Desh. Sheikh Mujibur Rehman found that there was very little room for manoeuvre left. While he was the foremost symbol of the autonomy movement, he was not its Jinnah. He was dispensable to the movement and he knew it. Therefore, he did not have the option to swim against the tide of popular opinion.

While the extreme left led by Mohammed Toaha, now organized into the Communist Party of East Pakistan (Marxist-Leninist) had broken away from the NAP (Bhashani group) on the issue of participation in the elections, thus weakening the NAP's electoral challenge to the Awami League, there was no evidence, except for a few posters advocating a revolution through bullets rather than the ballot, of any concerted drive by it to persuade the voters to refrain from going to the polls. One cannot also completely discount the possibility that the committee supporters of CPEP might have been directed to vote for the Awami League in order to give it as massive a mandate as possible. At any rate, any withdrawal of the left activists from the electoral arena would have left the Bengali voter with hardly any choice except to vote for the Awami League.

A massive victory for the Awami League was not seen as going against the long-term interests of the revolutionary left. It could count upon one of two eventualities which would then enable it to wrest the leadership of the province from the Awami League. First, if the Awami League succeeded in pushing through its six-point programme in full (which seemed unlikely) then it would have become the political and economic establishment of East Bengal which would of necessity have to maintain links and even a cordial working relationship with its counterpart in West Pakistan, both in the economic and political spheres. In addition to this, the character of the Awami League leadership and its reformist ideology made it clear to the Marxists that such a party, while it may be able to provide incentives to Bengali entrepreneurs in the cities, would not be able to solve the problems of the rural poor of the province. It would then be relatively easy for the revolutionary left to launch an attack on the new establishment, discredit it, and enlist mass support for a programme of radical change.

The second and more likely alternative was that the National Assembly would not accept the six-point programme in full because of the combined opposition of the army as well as the political forces representing West Pakistan. The Awami League would then be either left high and dry and proved ineffective or would compromise on the programme. In either case the revolutionary left would benefit. The ineffectiveness of leaders elected through the ballot-box would convince East Bengali opinion of the futility of such exercises. A revolutionary mood would emerge and the leadership would naturally gravitate to those committed to a violent overthrow of the existing order.

Taking into consideration all these factors it would seem that Sheikh Mujib's Awami League was the best bet for Islamabad. Unless accommodation was reached with it the situation in East Bengal would get out of Islamabad's hands not only in terms of the province's complete alienation from West Pakistan but also in terms of rapid radicalisation leading to a social upheaval in this entire region of the subcontinent. Therefore the League was the best bet from India's point of view also.

Unfortunately, the political environment in West Pakistan after the elections, plus the army's appreciation of its own narrow interests, precluded any accommodation with the Awami League which would satisfy East Bengali aspirations within the framework of Pakistan.

The emergence of the Pakistan People's Party (PPP) under Z. A. Bhutto as the strongest political force in West Pakistan, with commanding positions in the two most populous provinces of the West wing—Punjab and Sind—proved to be rather tragic as far as East Bengali aspirations are concerned. A politically splintered West Pakistan, unsure of itself, would not have been able to resist East Bengal's demands with the degree of confidence and stubbornness that it could show now.

Moreover, the army would not have been able to exploit such a situation to its advantage to the extent it could do as a result of the emergence of the PPP with a mandate which in effect neutralized the Awami League's victory in East Bengal. The PPP won almost 60 per cent of West Pakistan's seats in the National Assembly, including three-fourths of the seats from Punjab and two-thirds from Sind. It was not without reason that Bhutto, shortly after the elections, described these two provinces as the "bastions of power" in Pakistan.

The emergence of a strong West Pakistani party, with a flamboyant and strong-headed leader like Bhutto and with the right to speak for almost two-thirds of West Pakistan, seriously curtailed the Awami League's bargaining power. Thus, while the internal environment in East Bengal severely circumscribed the Awami League's freedom to manoeuver, the changes in the political environment in West Pakistan made it almost impossible that the Awami League's demands could be met to its satisfaction. All the elements of a deadlock were built into the situation.

That the interests of the army and those of the PPP converged as far as the inter-wing equation was concerned became very clear from the successive steps taken by both after the elections. It is interesting to note that Bhutto, who apparently rode to victory on the shoulders of his anti-establishment image, was very soon transformed into the darling of the establishment. This proved that at least in the short run there were no basic contradictions between the interests represented by these two forces. It should not be forgotten that Bhutto's anti-establishment image rested on the solid foundations of his anti-Tashkent image, which was popular with various quarters in the army. In fact, with the jettisoning of President Ayub, even the nominal commitment of the army to the Tashkent Declaration had come to an end.

The revanchist spirit of at least a section of the army leadership was well represented in the civilian sphere by Bhutto's mixture of irredentism and revanchism. East Bengali autonomy—both political and fiscal—while it threatened West Pakistani dominance, which was dear both to Bhutto and to the army, also threatened to upset the Indo-Pak equation in both military and political terms. This, once again, was equally unacceptable to both Bhutto and the army. The convergence of interests was, therefore, almost complete at least in this first stage of confrontation with East Bengal, though a later divergence could not be ruled out.

President Yahya Khan's position of assumed neutrality between the PPP and the Awami League during the initial stage of the constitutional parleys in effect helped the PPP. It gave Bhutto a veto over Pakistan's future constitutional and political progress. Bhutto put forward the "two majority parties" theory which was at first tacitly and then explicitly accepted by President Yahya Khan. This made it sure that no constitution could be framed or government installed without the PPP's participation and support. The Awami League's absolute majority in the National Assembly was, therefore, completely neutralized.

Once President Yahya Khan had declared his intention of granting Bhutto the right of veto over every constitutional formula, events in East Bengal took their logical course. The talks between Mujibur Rehman and Bhutto in the last week of January this year ended in deadlock primarily as a result of Bhutto's refusal to accept two of the Awami League's six points: that the powers of taxation and control of foreign exchange should be transferred to the provinces. Since they cut at the very roots of central control over financial resources and, therefore, its ability to maintain a large standing army, the two points were also completely unacceptable to the army. Moreover, it seems that Sheikh Mujibur Rehman made it very clear to Bhutto that under no circumstances would the Awami League be willing to share power with the PPP at the Centre. This, in effect, was a categorical rejection of the "two majority parties" theory put forward by the PPP leader.

It was no wonder that soon after these talks Bhutto started talking in terms of two Prime Ministers for Pakistan—one in the East and one in the West. Then again, the widely divergent stands of the two leaders on the issue of the hijacking of the Indian plane to Lahore, which incidentally synchronized with the failure of the Mujib-Bhutto talks, put the difference between their respective attitudes towards India into sharp focus and contributed to a widening of the gulf between the major political forces of the two wings.

The penultimate act in this tragic drama saw President Yahya Khan first summoning the Constituent-cum-National Assembly to meet in Dacca on March 3, and then, ostensibly under threat from Bhutto, postponing the session indefinitely. President Yahya Khan's announcement on March 1, postponing the session, was preceded by the PPP's decision to boycott the session and, if it was held without its participation, to launch a movement from "Khyber to Karachi" against the meeting of the Constituent Assembly. Bhutto contended that unless the Awami League declared categorically that the six points were not sacrosanct and that there was room for compromise and adjustment, the National Assembly would merely become an endorsing machinery for the Awami League programme which, in any case, was unacceptable to the PPP and by extension, to West Pakistan. Since such an assurance was not forthcoming from the Awami League, a complete deadlock ensued.

The convergence of the army's interests with those represented by Bhutto became crystal clear at this stage. The army seemed to be bent on delaying transfer of power to what it considered to be "unfriendly" civil hands and it was not averse to using Bhutto to achieve this end.

As far as East Bengal was concerned, President Yahya Khan's decision to postpone the session of the Constituent Assembly was the proverbial last straw that broke the camel's back. The Awami League leadership had been under constant pressure not to compromise with the military junta. Sheikh Mujib's relatively conciliatory policy began to lose ground under the pressure of events. By postponing the Assembly session, President Yahya Khan, representing the West Pakistani establishment, had made it very clear, with the whole-hearted support of the new West Pakistani political elite represented by Bhutto, that Dacca would not be allowed to rule from Islamabad. The Awami League's thesis that as the largest party in Pakistan, with an absolute majority in the National Assembly, it had the right to mould the future constitutional and political set-up according to its policy and programme was thus blown to pieces. The foremost advocates and defenders of Pakistan's unity and integrity dealt the death blow to the very concept of Pakistan by refusing to accord the Awami League the status of the majority party in the all-Pakistan context.

On March 1, the six-point programme of the Awami League passed into history. Having been denied the right to rule from Islamabad, the Awami League's strategy shifted beyond the

six-point programme to an even more loosely knit confederation where it would be really immaterial as to who ruled at
the centre. But before we discuss this shift in the Awami
League's strategy a word is necessary about the instantaneous
and spontaneous East Bengali reaction to the postponement of
the proposed Assembly session. Even before a coordinated
strategy of a civil disobedience movement could be chalked
out by the Awami League, students and others had taken
to the streets to demonstrate against what they considered to
be fresh evidence of the regime's duplicity. This resulted in
police and military firings in which several people lost their
lives. The Awami League had to fall in line and the call was
given for a non-violent non-cooperation movement. This was
another instance of the Awami League being led by public
opinion instead of leading it. The response to the call for civil
disobedience was fantastic and surpassed anything seen before.
From the highest to the lowest in the land, non-cooperation
with the military authorities was complete. This was evidence,
if it was still needed, that the East Bengalis were now a nation.

With the situation getting out of control to an extent not
envisaged by Islamabad, and with the West Pakistani army
holed up in cantonments and deprived of even basic and essential services, President Yahya Khan flew into Dacca on March
15 to hold talks with Sheikh Mujibur Rehman ostensibly to
find a way out of this impasse. Earlier, President Yahya Khan
had convened a meeting of political leaders of both wings
for March 10 but this attempt turned out to be abortive because the Awami League rejected the President's invitation.
This forced General Yahya Khan to go on the air on March 6
and, in an effort to pacify East Bengali opinion, call the Constituent Assembly back into session on March 25.

But such gestures were no longer adequate to assuage East
Bengali feelings. East Bengal's faith in the impartiality of
President Yahya Khan had ceased to exist. Sheikh Mujibur
Rehman put forward four pre-conditions for the Awami
League's participation in the Constituent Assembly session
which was now proposed. These four conditions were: an
immediate end to martial law, withdrawal of troops to the
barracks, restoration of civilian rule and an inquiry into the
killing of East Bengali civilians by the military since the
beginning of the non-cooperation movement.

This brings us back to the shift in the Awami League strategy after March 1. What the Awami League wanted now was immediate transfer of power to its hands in East Bengal and the withdrawal of the military from the arena of civilian administration, first to its barracks and ultimately to West Pakistan. The Awami League, now convinced that it would not be allowed to rule Islamabad, wanted at least to rule Dacca in order to conserve East Bengal's resources (since a transfer of resources from West to East Pakistan was not permitted) and channelise them exclusively for East Bengal's development.

Complete independence was probably still not contemplated. What the Awami League wanted now was some sort of a loose confederation which would let the legal entity called Pakistan continue but at the same time transfer effective control of East Bengal to Bengali hands with the minimum of interference from Islamabad. In fact, in order to present General Yahya Khan with a *fait accompli,* Sheikh Mujibur Rehman announced on the day the President was scheduled to arrive in Dacca, that he was taking over the civil administration of the province. He also issued 35 directives setting out the guidelines according to which the civil administration was to operate.

It is easy to say with hindsight that President Yahya Khan during his 11-day stay in Dacca and during his negotiations with Sheikh Mujibur Rehman was buying time for the six ships-load of troops from Karachi to reach Chittagong. But during the time the Yahya-Mujib talks were going on there was an air of optimism both in Dacca and outside that seems to have been unreal and devoid of any substance. President Yahya Khan's decision to institute an inquiry into the incidents of military-civilian clashes added to the optimism. In fact as late as March 24, the AFP correspondent in Dacca was quoting an "impeccable source" as telling him that President Yahya Khan was going to proclaim virtual autonomy for East Pakistan under a new Pakistan confederation within 24 hours and that a draft copy of this proclamation which was prepared by President Yahya Khan's advisers was returned to the President by the Awami League headquarters with only technical amendments. This was one reason why, when the hour of the actual showdown arrived, both the people of East Bengal as well as the world outside were taken by surprise. It should, however, be noted that even while the negotiations were going on serious clashes had taken place between the West Pakistani army and the Bengali civil resisters in Chittagong, Saidpur and Joidevpur.

According to President Yahya Khan's broadcast of March 26, the talks broke down over Sheikh Mujibur Rehman's insistence that the Constituent Assembly should first meet in two sections representing the two wings, work out two separate constitutions for their wings and then meet in joint session to frame a constitution for the confederation. This was not acceptable to West Pakistani politicians, primarily Bhutto, who were also in Dacca during the last three or four days of negotiations. But the President's version remains to be corroborated by any other reliable source.

One can go on speculating endlessly about President Yahya Khan's motives in launching the brutal suppression on the night of March 25-26 without even a prior acknowledgement that the negotiations had failed. One can, of course, with Peter Preston of the *Guardian*, call it "the act of a mindless sergeant-major" and leave it at that. But it was not all that simple. There is enough evidence now at least to assume that the army high command, in collusion with Bhutto, had come to the conclusion soon after the elections that power would be transferred to an Awami League-dominated civilian government only when they were assured that the six points were suitably whittled down so as not to threaten their vital interests. Once it became clear that this was not possible due to the inner compulsion of East Bengali politics as well as the magnitude of East Bengal's revulsion against "alien" domination, the rest—the postponement of the Assembly and the brutal massacre—followed logically.

What the ruling junta had failed to anticipate was the magnitude of the East Bengal response to such strong-arm tactics. This miscalculation cost them dearly. Not only did it force the military rulers to unleash a wave of brutal repression which finally buried, though not very neatly, the concept of Pakistan, it also had the potential of letting loose forces in the region which may well pave the way for an unprecedented social upheaval at least in this part of the sub-continent. West Pakistan itself, though geographically isolated from East Bengal, will not be able to escape the long-term effects of such an upheaval. In fact, the serious drain on the West

Pakistani economy, which will be unavoidable if the army of occupation in East Bengal is to be maintained at a reasonable level of efficiency, may create problems for the army in its own home base, West Pakistan, which had not been envisaged earlier.

It is difficult to hazard a guess at this juncture as to the future character of the East Bengal resistance movement. But there are a few things which are becoming clear. First, the struggle is going to be a long drawn out one and will have to be waged by the freedom fighters primarily with indigeneous support, both in terms of human and material resources. Second, the resistance movement is, therefore, bound to take on the character of guerrilla warfare. Third, and this is a corollary to the second point, the leadership of such a movement can be reasonably expected to pass into the hands of people well-versed, relatively speaking, both in the theory and practice of guerrilla warfare. This does not mean that the movement would lose the wide nationalist support it has. East Bengal's resentment against domination by West Pakistan is too strong for the movement to lose its wide nationalist support base. But the actual organisation, operation and leadership of the movement would come to be concentrated in the hands of a dedicated band of hard core guerrilla leaders with a future-oriented messianic ideology to keep them fighting against heavy odds.

Fourth, instead of operating on a number of very wide fronts separated from each other, as the Mukti Fouj had done during the initial stages of uncoordinated fighting, the guerrilla movement would spread slowly but surely from a secure base which would be under the firm control of the liberation forces. This central base of operations is likely to be located somewhere in the northern portion of Bangla Desh where the main strength of the Marxist cadres is concentrated. Fifth, the leadership of East Bengal, which had been primarily concentrated since 1947 in the central and southern districts of the province, that is Dacca and the areas around it, may shift to northern Bengal and may thus redress some of the imbalance in the political structure within Bangla Desh. Sixth, remnants of the East Pakistan Rifles and the East Bengal Regiment who have so far formed the nucleus of the Mukti Fouj may for some time present an alternative leadership to the Marxist element but it is more likely than not that they will be gradually assimilated into the general political culture of the guerrilla movement.

But all this is largely in the nature of crystal gazing. One thing is, however, very clear. Even though West Pakistan succeeds in keeping large parts of East Bengal under its occupation for some time, Pakistan as conceived by Jinnah is dead and without any possibility of resurrection. Artificial respiration may keep it going for some time but the process will turn out to be so painful and so expensive that Islamabad will be forced in the short rather than the long run to withdraw its occupation forces from Bangla Desh.

INTO BATTLE—UNARMED

COL. R. RAMA RAO (RETD.)

THE WAR unleashed by Pakistan on the unarmed and innocent people of Bangla Desh is not a rebellion organised by a few 'miscreants' as General Yahya Khan would like the world to believe, or even a civil war as referred to by some foreign observers. It is a national war of liberation by 75 million people, who have discovered their identity and are determined to free themselves from colonial exploitation.

Pakistan's military machine has traditionally been trained, equipped and positioned so as to be able to carry out a fairly wide spectrum of operations against India—especially in and around Jammu and Kashmir and on India's western borders generally. But on the eastern side its strategy was to position a relatively small sized force in East Bengal whose main purpose was to buttress the local administration. Until 1965, only one infantry division was stationed there, along with units of East Pakistan Rifles and armed police, which however, were officered predominantly by West Pakistanis.

More recently, the regular garrisons in East Bengal were reinforced by a second infantry division. The East Bengal Regiment, whose nucleus was formed shortly after the partition, was further strengthened and additional battalions of East Pakistan Rifles were raised. Broadly this was the position in December last, when East Bengal gave an astonishing display of national solidarity and within the framework of a peaceful and democratic process conferred upon Sheikh Mujibur Rehman's Awami League an almost unanimous mandate for complete internal autonomy.

Sizeable elements in East Bengal were for immediate and undiluted independence but Sheikh Mujibur Rehman persuaded the people of Bangla Desh to accept a united Pakistan in which there would be complete internal autonomy for East Bengal and the central government would have clearly defined powers; his purpose was to ensure a peaceful settlement of constitutional issues. But the unity and steadfastness of the people of Bangla Desh so frightened the military junta and professional India baiters in Islamabad that they unleashed an operation which has jeopardised the future of Pakistan. Its savagery has done long-term damage to Bangla Desh as also to West Pakistan itself.

The nationalists were caught unprepared by this brutal onslaught. They, and especially the Awami League which by its sustained work in the country for over two decades had taken the message of autonomy to the people, had concentrated entirely on attaining their goals by peaceful methods. They had never thought of preparing themselves for the savagery which was let loose upon them in a sudden and premeditated move; hence the severe losses they suffered in leadership and the physical destruction of the assets of the country.

The overall aim of the Pakistan army's Operation "Massacre" in Bangla Desh was to force the "problem of East Pakistan" "to a final solution" as General Tikka Khan was believed to have stated, through cold-blooded savagery, organised killings, and the ruthless use of all the elements of the military power of state by a minority against the peaceful majority of what it claimed to be its own population. The plan was to kill, in one sweep, all the leaders, present and potential, of Bangla Desh so that the shock of the mass killings and the absence of leadership among the nationalists may cow down the population into submission. After that, further extermination of Bengali nationalists and members of the minority community could be undertaken at leisure so as to fulfil

General Tikka Khan's stated objective of reducing Bengalis from a numerical majority in Pakistan as they were at the beginning of the Ides of March, to a minority before the slaughter was called off.

But the plan did not succeed. Although West Pakistani soldiers armed with tanks, heavy guns, mortars, automatics and attacking aircraft mowed down at least 300,000 people in 48 hours, significant sections of popular leadership survived the treacherous attack. At the same time the Army failed to gain assured control of even the principal cities and towns despite several days of fighting in which it had the advantage of fire power, mobility, organisational facilities, command and control structures, and above all resources, initiative and premeditation. This is a measure of the failure of planning on the part of General Abdul Hamid the Army Chief, Gen. Gul Hassan, his Director of Planning and Operations and Gen. Peerzada the power behind the throne. It is also a measure of the failure of Gen. Tikka Khan the local 'gaulitier' who was confident of crushing East Bengal in 48 hours. This failure has forced a change of plans in the Pakistan army which is evident from the course of operations during the first four weeks, which can be reviewed in five phases.

The first, or the preparatory phase, could be said to have formally begun shortly after Sheikh Mujibur Rehman emerged as the undisputed leader of East Bengal, if not of the whole of Pakistan as it then was, and took his uncompromising stand on complete internal autonomy for East Bengal. At this stage, the hawks in the army began to evolve plans for holding Bengal by the sword in the event of failure of political moves to deny autonomy to the eastern wing. These plans involved moving the equivalent of the striking elements of two infantry divisions into East Bengal, stockpiling ammunition and stores, re-positioning the garrisons suitably for the ensuing operations and above all discreetly separating Bengali officers and men from 'pure' Pakistanis and, as far as possible, disarming Bengali units of the regular army, the East Bengal Regiment and East Pakistan Rifles.

This treacherous move went practically unnoticed since there were few senior Bengali officers in the army and fewer still in positions either at Army Headquarters or in any formation headquarters for that matter. Those Bengali officers who were in positions where the tension of the impending events could be sensed were dealt with either by treachery or by strong arm methods. Brigadier Muzumdar, in command at Chittagong, was arrested and shot. Major Khaled Musharaff, now commanding Mukti Fouj in the eastern sector was despatched from his headquarters on a phoney errand. Thirty-five Bengali officers of the East Bengal Regiment and 200 of their men were treacherously attacked at night by their erstwhile colleagues and machine gunned. So were many policemen and men of the East Pakistan Rifles at Dacca and other centres.

By February 20 it was perhaps clear to the hawks in the army that there was no prospect of persuading East Bengali leadership to compromise on the issue of autonomy. Hence they had, as they saw it, the choice of letting East Bengal assert its full autonomy, thus deflating the central government of Pakistan, which meant the army itself, or of making a well planned and determined move to crush East Bengal for ever. This was the so called 'final solution' for East Bengal, which was eventually accepted for implementation. Accordingly, secret preparations for reinforcing the east wing garrisons and stockpiling maintenance stores were completed. While these were under implementation, Gen. Yahya Khan, under threat of overthrow by Gen. Abdul Hamid and others, engaged Mujibur Rehman in long drawn out parleys. Many subterfuges were employed by the army to lull the victims into a false sense of security. Notable among these were the series of communiques and inspired leaks as late as March 24 which gave the impression that Gen. Yahya Khan and the Awami League leadership were about to reach a political settlement and all would be well thereafter.

The second or the decapitation phase was the key feature of the operations and nothing was left to chance in carrying it out. Tanks, guns and mortars and infantry armed with machine guns were positioned at points especially chosen for destruction—the hostels and halls of residence of Dacca University; Dhanmandi, the residential district where Sheikh Mujibur Rehman lived; the city area where members of the minority community lived; the offices of newspapers and the main city centre. At the precise hour, unsuspecting people were shelled and machine-gunned to death. Before daybreak, tens of thousands—mostly the intelligentsia of Dacca—had been decimated, that is those who failed to escape to safety earlier that day. The same fate overtook policemen at some of the police stations of Dacca and the Bengali elements of the East Pakistan Rifles and units of the East Bengal Regiment where Bengali officers had failed to take anticipatory action. As in Dacca, the army swooped down on sleeping citizens in Comilla, Jessore and Rangpur. In Chittagong the army had killed several thousands a couple of days earlier in what was a dress-rehearsal for Operation Massacre.

But this phase of the operation proved to be a failure. A good percentage of Bengali leadership was wiped out but a sufficiently large percentage managed to escape. After the initial shock wore out villagers in outlying areas rallied round local police, Awami League and National Awami Party volunteers to surround isolated army garrisons and inflict punishment on them. Nationalist volunteers also cut roads and telegraph wires between Dacca and other towns and paralysed communications. There is evidence to show that in this phase Pakistani forces, carried away by their own savagery, fired indiscriminately and consumed far more ammunition than the prevailing circumstances allowed or the results justified.

The third phase aimed at occupation. After the mass murders in Dacca and the main garrison cities, Pakistani troops could claim that they had established 'control' over the cities by shooting down Bengalis at sight, holding the airfields at Dacca and Sandwip Island and the ports of Chittagong and Chalna, and so permitting the use of aircraft for inter-wing movement of a military nature. The next phase was strengthening outposts and reinforcing dispersed garrisons. Here the Pakistani armed forces sustained casualties but also killed thousands of innocent Bengalis, especially professionals, young men and school and college boys.

Reinforcements were airlifted to garrisons except where the army, as at and around Rangpur and in the Dacca and Tangail area, was in a position to use tanks to spearhead an advance. In the initial stages troops were reckless with their ammunition. Subsequently, however, by using informers and spies and adopting ruses to gather Bangalis around them, the troops mowed down thousands in sharp killing sprees. Shocked by their colossal losses, nationalists learnt to be wary of the tactics of deception adopted by Pakistani soldiers and the treachery of local non-Bengali elements. They avoided frontal assaults even on isolated garrisons and learnt that ambushes and disruption of supply and troop movements paid better dividends.

This phase of operations may be said to have been completed with the army regaining control of Kushtia, Dinajpur and Rajshahi in the west, Lalmonirhat in the north and other towns in the Central Zone. In the eastern sector as well as in the western sector the army was still encountering stiff resistance and suffering losses. That did not, however, prevent it from starting the next phase of operations, the expansion phase.

With the end of the task of reinforcing selected garrisons, the army has been trying to improve its lines of communication in order to fan out into the surrounding areas and improve its control there. Many surface communications, that is road and rail links, are still disrupted, and since there is no prospect of these being restored for uninterrupted use even by the army for quite some time, the army is unlikely to expend resources in either material or manpower to get them going. The headquarters at Dacca is maintaining its links, such as they are, with outlying garrisons by air for transporting reinforcements and replenishments and by wireless for communications. In addition it is maintaining garrisons by inland waterways. In selected stretches of the country, overland contact with garrisons is being maintained by armoured columns which are also ideal for terrorising and subduing the people and wiping out pockets of resistance. Reinforcements of tanks have been coming in from West Pakistan for this purpose. So, presumably, are light naval craft for intercommunication duties and troop and freight movements.

The monsoons will no doubt, circumscribe support and maintenance operations by air. But ground operations cannot be ruled out. By more extensive use of spies, informers, and fifth columnists the army could move in platoon and company strength to selected points and kill large bodies of innocent and unsuspecting people. The strategy would be to continue to wipe out Bengali-speaking people, especially the middle-classes and skilled workers, so that the army would encounter at the end no opposition whatsoever.

There remains, however, the problem of sealing the 2500 km long land frontier with India which would make serious demands on the army. This is a formidable task. Pakistan is not likely to underestimate its magnitude as it moves on to the final or consolidation phase. During this phase, the West Pakistani army hopes a cowed down population would submit tamely to West Pakistani rule. West Pakistanis could utilise the 'locals' as slaves to carry out their behests and lead a sub-human existence. As a West Punjabi major gloated before an American citizen in Chittagong, "no Bengali would drive a car. Only we, West Pakistanis, and foreigners would own or drive cars". The major also mentioned other things which would cause revulsion among civilised people.

Normally, for a 70,000 to 80,000 strong force logistic support to the extent of 400 tons a day would be needed. Pakistani armed forces, however, cannot be judged by the standards of other armies. Looting the Bengali population has become the standard method with it for obtaining milk, meat, vegetables and grain. This no doubt would mean a somewhat uncertain quality and unbalanced rations, but rapacious local commanders would make up for it by increased lootings. With the problem of rations thus solved, logistic support would only mean the supply of weapons and equipment spares and replacement spares and fuel for vehicles and ammunition. To this must be added casualty evacuation and essential troop reinforcements. On this basis a total lift of about 300 tons a day would be needed, 200 tons for maintenance and the remainder for essential personnel movement and unforeseen needs. With its existing air- and sea-lift facilities, Pakistan would be able to meet this commitment indefinitely. It can thus bear the direct costs of the operations for some time.

But the indirect costs, especially of a prolonged war, would be extremely high since even during the short period of the first one month, the physical assets of East Bengal in the shape of road and rail bridges and transport facilities were destroyed. A number of workshops and some at least of the factories have been damaged, production of jute and tea has been dislocated. Thus the capacity of East Bengal to earn foreign exchange has been seriously hurt. East Bengal will no longer be an asset to Pakistan unless West Pakistan invests heavily in rehabilitating the country. This brings out the futility of the entire operation. The army found it necessary to destroy the country in order to hold it, and then to make it worthwhile for the army and West Pakistan to continue to hold it, a heavy cost has to be met for re-building its physical assets and economic structure which were devastated overnight.

This is the background against which the outlook for the future has to be assessed. To start with, the nationalists could not take the initiative because the army, after secretly preparing its plan and completing the necessary preliminary moves, struck suddenly at an hour of its choosing while the leaders of the nationalist movement had deliberately confined themselves to constitutional methods for attaining their political objectives. The nationalists were largely unaware of the power of organised forces and the damage they could cause.

Fortunately, at least half the officer ranks of the Bengali element of Bengal Regiment, the East Pakistan Rifles and local police survived and were able to quickly group themselves in an ad hoc manner in order to organise resistance in some sectors at least. Almost overnight they built up resistance groups throughout the country with Awami League and National Awami Party volunteers.

But the circumstances under which the resistance groups sprang up compelled them to operate more or less on their own. They were ill-armed, indeed, mostly unarmed, and found themselves left only to their own resources, unable physically to offer coherent opposition to the occupation forces. Timely help was of the essence. They badly needed arms, logistic support and above all, means for establishing direct and reliable channels of communication between the four sectors in which the resistance forces have grouped themselves. While in all partisan wars, liberation forces have generally been able to secure the bulk of their requirements from the enemy, there has been no case where they have been successful without some outside assistance, especially in the initial stages. Mukti Fouj men, unable to secure such help, were unable to regroup and reorganise themselves effectively to consolidate the areas in which they had won some initial control. By operating in small, well-organised groups they tried to deal with the occupation army's garrisons so long as these were isolated; they could take advantage of their local knowledge as they tried to intercept the army's movements over waterways, damaging his equipment for mobility, which is more difficult to replace than soldiery. Obviously the strategy of the Mukti Fouj, in so far as there was any careful strategy behind its isolated actions, was that once its outpost garrisons were destroyed, the Pakistan army would be confined to the Chittagong-Dacca sector and the Chalna port area, and gradually the inexorable pressure of events would drive it out of Bangla Desh. But in the nearly total absence of the vital minimum outside assistance which it needed, the Mukti Fouj could not carry out the strategy. External assistance to Pakistan would perhaps be forthcoming from China and its CENTO/RCD partners. China has already affirmed its support to Pakistan and warned India of dire consequences in the event of this country "interfering in the internal affairs of Pakistan" This is really a message to Pakistan that it can take a calculated risk in denuding its garrisons in West Pakistan in order to reinforce its army in the East. Pakistan has indeed already taken this risk, because it cannot support action on any scale in the East once there is any trouble in the West.

China has reportedly promised military equipment for any forces that Pakistan may raise in the West wing in replacement of forces transferred to East Bengal. This according to some observers, is taken to mean that Pakistan has asked for and China has agreed to provide equipment for a new infantry and an armoured division being raised in West Pakistan. Another report credits China with having assured Pakistan that she would provide Pakistan with all the arms and military equipment she needs. She has also promised economic aid to the tune of Rs. 20 crores immediately.

Pakistan, however, has some immediate problems, particularly in the matter of re-structuring her air and naval forces. This need arises from the fact that, relatively speaking, her navy and air force has had a fair proportion of East Bengali technicians. Following the army's reign of terror in East Bengal, Bengali sailors and airmen who were in West Pakistan became 'enemy personnel' overnight. A number have been liquidated. Some perhaps have deserted while the rest have been held under custody by the military regime.

Apparently, Pakistan's military planners failed to take due note of the fact that in certain key branches of the navy and air force—including communications and maintenance—a significant proportion of tradesmen were Bengalis. Nor, have outside observers discerned its true significance in the present context. It is brought out in the following table:

Proportion of Bengalis in the Services

	Army	Navy	Air Force
Officers	5%	10%	16%
Branch Officers	NA	5%	NA
JCOS/Warrant Officers/ Chief Petty Officers	7.5%	10.4%	17%
Petty Officers	NA	17.3%	—
Other Ranks	7.5%	28.8%	30%

(NA + Not applicable)

This was the position in 1963-64. Subsequently, Pakistan's armed forces were expanded considerably. In the Ayub regime an attempt was made to induct more Bengalis. Since the fall of Ayub, East Bengal's share of vacancies in the armed forces has possibly fallen. But even taking the above as the basis for examining the operational efficiency and battle-worthiness of Pakistan's armed forces, especially its navy and air force, some significant conclusions can be drawn.

Bengali officers of Pakistan's army have either been killed, arrested on trumped up charges, or put into harmless positions in the western wing.. Those who are free, are fighting for their country in Bangla Desh. This applies equally to Bengali other ranks of the army. Likewise, naval officers and ratings in East Bengal, barring those in Chalna and Chittagong, have been killed or are fighting as part of Mukti Fouj. Still substantial elements—say about 15 per cent—of the personnel of naval units and establishments in West Pakistan, as on March 25, were probably Bengalis. They must have been arrested but they must be replaced before Pakistan's navy can be put to sea. Those conversant with armed forces' training would appreciate that a unit with about 15 per cent deficiency in strength is less than 75 per cent battle-worthy.

In the case of Pakistan's air force, the position is even more serious. Almost 30 per cent of the other rank strength is of Bengalis. Barring perhaps two squadrons, the entire air force is in the western wing and it cannot be sustained in the air with 25 per cent to 30 per cent of its air crew treated as suspect. Perhaps they are being replaced. But an airman cannot be trained overnight. Until the Bengali airmen who were killed or confined to lines in West Pakistan are replaced by trained men the battle-worthiness of Pakistan's air force is unlikely to be more than 65 per cent to 75 per cent of its rated value. This no doubt can change in the next four to six months. But during these six months Pakistan is more vulnerable than her military planners apparently realised. Until after the shots were fired, Pakistan's army chief failed to appreciate the significance of this point. The urgent importunations to Turkish and Iranian air and naval chiefs, would have been to obtain maintenance cover for Pakistan's air and naval fleets from these countries in this critical period.

Apart from the fall in the operational effectiveness of its navy and air force arising from the alienation of East Bengalis in these services, Pakistan made a strategic mistake in opening the campaign on the lines it chose to. Chairman Mao—the mentor of Pakistan's army leaders—had declared in his treatise on "Protracted War" that he would unhesitatingly accept battle where victory was certain; would avoid battle where victory was uncertain and would absolutely decline battle if battle placed the future of the country at stake. This last is precisely what Yahya Khan and his commanders have done.

The major powers have had ample time to study what has happened in Bangla Desh, assess their long-term interests and chart out their courses of action. The super powers as well as China and Britain could influence events substantially. The USSR has made no secret of its sympathies and has called on Yahya Khan to settle the issue peacefully. While not willing to take the initiative in recognising Bangla Desh, it would probably fall in line if those having a greater stake in the matter took action. The USA has decided to wait and see. Despite the influential pro-Pakistani school of thought at the middle level in the Pentagon and State Department, officially the USA is not overcommitted to Pakistan. Intellectuals and liberals have unequivocally come out in favour of democracy and against military brutality and genocide. For this opinion to assert itself, time is needed. Meanwhile if some other source which is not unfriendly to the USA assists Bangla Desh, American opinion is unlikely to be averse to this, and indeed it may choose to support such a venture, discreetly at any rate.

China has come out firmly on the side of Pakistan's ruling junta. It is not unlikely, that China's policy is to see that whatever the outcome in East Bengal, West Pakistan, with or without East Bengal, should remain firmly tied to Peking. At the appropriate time, China could woo East Bengal, so China's strategists may argue. Britain's official stand seems to be to support Islamabad's military regime. Its argument seems to be that Britain's assets in East Bengal are perhaps as good as gone. Hence expediency demands friendliness with West Pakistan to protect British assets in that wing at least and also to extract appropriate political and economic advantages for the support now extended.

THE STRATEGIC FALL-OUT

BRIG. RATHY SAWHNY (RETD.)

DIFFERENCES OF opinion of course can and do exist over the likely outcome of the current freedom struggle in East Bengal. However, one thing is certain—the old Pakistan is dead and buried under a mountain of corpses even though its military rulers seem frantically to be attempting to deny this self-evident fact through massive and savage military repression. And even if West Pakistan were to succeed in crushing the liberation struggle for any length of time and in reimposing what could now be nothing short of nakedly exposed colonial rule over an unwilling East Bengal, the resultant entity inevitably would be vastly different from the erstwhile national state of Pakistan.

To bring into correct perspective the strategic possibilities inherent in the currently developing situation it is necessary to examine briefly the previous situation and the relevance of military power in this day and age.

The instability which in the past has plagued this sub-continent has been due very largely to a misconceived attempt on the part of the Western powers, particularly the U.S.A., to create an artificial balance of power between India and Pakistan, by giving the latter massive, free military aid as well as economic assistance. China and the Soviet Union, by providing military assistance to Pakistan, further contributed to the "balance" contrived by the West. But recent events in East Bengal have shattered the credibility of this unnatural balance once and for all, and this has coincided with a strengthening of India's own power potential as a result of the clear-cut mandate Mrs. Gandhi's leadership secured in the nation-wide democratic elections. Willy-nilly, India has become the pre-eminent national power in the Asian region south of the Himalayan crests, a position which is no more than commensurate with this country's geo-strategic location and her human and material resources.

Military power certainly is no longer if it ever was, the exclusive ingredient of a nation's total power. Before the nuclear era it was perhaps the predominant element when it was by and large the concentrated expression of the might of the state. Even in those days a nation's power potential was significantly influenced by its economic, political and social structure, but these aspects were considered to be additional to the purely military factors. But after World War II, with the emergence of two super powers, each heading its own power bloc, the influence of various factors in the balance of power changed to some extent in favour of the non-military factors. Military power began to lose its effectiveness as a means of putting pressure on an opponent. The war in Vietnam has demonstrated the limitations on the application of military might. Two factors have significantly contributed to this state of affairs. First, the widespread diffusion of arms and the comparative ease with which weapons, ammunition and other war materials can now be inducted into an area of conflict. Second, the vast increase in the flow of information, news and propaganda that has been made possible by improved means of communication. The cost of exploiting occupied territory has greatly increased, and there is now a wide spectrum of resistance techniques, from going slow and sabotage through kidnapping and hijacking to full scale guerrilla war; so a determined people can make the occupier's costs rise above his benefits.

The destruction of one's enemy for self-defence can no longer be the aim of strategy, and even the enforced disarming of another nation through the destruction of its armed forces has become a meaningless concept in the international sphere, except perhaps when one super power disarms a much weaker nation and the other super power accepts the situation at least tacitly because it believes the victim is outside its own sphere of influence.

Although technically the liberation struggle in East Bengal is perhaps an intra-national as opposed to an international conflict, the uniqueness of Pakistan, with its two constituent wings separated by 1200 miles of Indian territory, as well as the ethnic, economic and political differences between them gives this conflict most if not all the essential characteristics of a war between two nations. And this is especially so in view of the fact that India, which is East Bengal's only immediate neighbour and whose territory surrounds East Bengal on three sides, has proclaimed her sympathy and support for the people of East Bengal.

The military capabilities of the two sides, the course the operations have so far taken and how the situation is likely to develop are aspects of the Bangla Desh movement which are covered elsewhere in this volume. Here an attempt will be made to evaluate India's geo-strategic stakes, political and military, in the three different types of situation that could conceivably result from the current conflict if:

(a) West Pakistan succeeds in effectively suppressing the liberation movement in, say, less than six months;

(b) East Bengal wins either complete independence or a substantial degree of autonomy in less than six months; and

(c) a stalemate is reached with neither side conclusively able to win despite a prolonged war.

Even in the unlikely event of West Pakistan succeeding in putting it down, the freedom movement would be most unlikely to die out, since the freedom fighters would certainly be able to avail of sanctuaries across the border and would continue to receive the sympathy and support of the people of India. The Pakistanis would therefore have to hold down and administer East Bengal with an army of occupation, which would constantly face smouldering hatred and periodic flare-ups of open hostility, which would probably grow progressively stronger. A large part of East Bengal's limited industrial base has already been systematically destroyed by the Pakistani soldiers, and it is being damaged further every day. In the circumstances neither West Pakistani nor foreign capital will be forthcoming for investment in the disturbed region, and consequently the rehabilitation of East Bengal's industry and economy will be a painfully slow process. Foreign powers like the U.S.A. which have large foodgrain surpluses crowding their warehouses, will probably be ready to pour in relief shipments as soon as adequate unloading and transport facilities are restored. Agricultural production, particularly of rice, could probably be restored fairly soon. But the impoverished state of the industrial workers and the urban population as well as strong anti-Punjabi sentiments would prevent East Bengal from providing lucrative and protected market again for the produce of West Pakistan industry, a point more fully discussed in a later section by an economist with a specialised interest in Pakistan. By and large therefore, even if West Pakistan succeeds in regaining control, holding down East Bengal as an unwilling partner will prove more of a liability than an asset in restoring Pakistan's overall national power to its former level.

If, as seems most probable, East Bengal eventually wins complete independence or a substantial degree of autonomy, it will not only directly reduce Pakistan's over-all power but will also have other serious repercussions in the eastern wing which will further diminish its power potential. The reduction would be greatest if East Bengal became independent. Pakistan would, in that case, also lose the distinction of being the largest Muslim nation; its population would be smaller than the number of Muslims in India. But even if Pakistan becomes a loose federation, its power would fall drastically because the resources of East Bengal would no longer be so readily available as in the past to sustain large West Pakistani armed forces.

According to official figures Pakistan's defence budget amounted to about 3.6 per cent of its GNP in 1970-71. But its defence expenditure is probably not fully reflected in the defence budget and it can be assumed to be about 6 per cent of the GNP. The current fighting will increase the defence burden in this and subsequent years because wastages will have to be replaced and reserve stocks of ammunition and equipment built up. With the loss of foreign exchange earnings and the protected East Bengal market, West Pakistan's economy will be in trouble, and even assuming a large-scale increase in trade with and aid from China, it will be difficult for Pakistan to afford to spend the 12 per cent or so of its reduced GNP which it would need to spend to maintain its military confrontation with India at the previous level.

Since a truncated Pakistan would no longer be able to provide credible countervailing power *vis-a-vis* India, the incentive for foreign powers, including China, to build up Pakistan's military power to its previous level would be considerably reduced. It would also be extremely difficult for Pakistan to muster support at world forums for its now even more blatantly unjustified attitude over Kashmir; with the brutal genocide it has unleashed upon its own unarmed Bengali Muslim citizens, West Pakistan has shattered Jinnah's two-nation theory which was based on religion and used to be invoked by Pakistan to buttress its claim on Kashmir. These developments will inevitably have a strong impact on the internal situation in West Pakistan itself, where the Baluchis, Pathans and Sindhis will probably demand more autonomy for themselves. It will thus become more and more difficult for Pakistan's rulers to compel their people to make sacrifices for an attempt, which it is quite evident is becoming increasingly more futile, to alter the *status quo* on the sub-continent through resort to military force against India.

It has been suggested in some quarters that Pakistan's military rulers, having recognised that East Bengal will eventually slip out of their control, have opted in a somewhat Machaevellian fashion and perhaps under Chinese tuition for a protracted struggle so as to ensure that an extreme leftist leadership— preferably China-oriented—and not Sheikh Mujib's more moderate Awami League should inherit power in the region; the former would prove a thorn in India's side and thus to some extent offset the shift in the balance of power. But this is not likely to happen.

While it is evident that the Pakistanis have made every effort to decimate the Awami League leadership and also intellectuals and administrative cadres, it is becoming increasingly clear that they have not succeeded to the extent that was earlier feared. The overwhelming support of the Bengali masses which the Awami League had enjoyed remains in tact. On the contrary, the fact that its leaders have been singled out as the special target by the hated West Pakistani forces has probably enhanced the Awami League's standing. Left-wing leaders including Maulana Bhashani, Toaha and others have openly thrown in their lot with the Awami League in the common struggle for liberation.

Even conceding that a protracted war might throw up a new set of resistance leaders with extremist views, it does not automatically follow that this development would be disastrous for India. It would be suicidal for even Maoist Bengalis to adopt a pro-Peking line in the face of the support which China has openly proclaimed for the West Pakistani military regime in its brutal suppression of the freedom movement. A volte-face on China's part cannot be entirely ruled out. However, it will be difficult for it to live down the stab in the back which it has inflicted on the Bengali national liberation movement.

Somewhat exaggerated fears have also been expressed about the possibilities of a spill over of extremist elements from East to West Bengal, and even of resurgent Bengali nationalism inducing an already turbulent West Bengal to detach itself from India to join East Bengal to form an independent nation, with Assam possibly included in it. Adherents of this view seem to have lost sight of the fact that East Bengali Muslims are unlikely to want to liberate themselves from West Pakistani Muslim domination merely to exchange it for domination by West Bengal Hindus. Perhaps those hypnotised by the separation thesis will soon start conjuring up the danger that linguistic and cultural affinity will also persuade Punjabis in West Pakistan and neighbouring areas of India to demand a separate nation for themselves.

Prolongation of the conflict is certainly undesirable; it goes against humanitarian considerations as well as India's interests. It will make the refugee problem, serious already, still more serious for India, and particularly for West Bengal which is already very densely populated. There is also the danger that Pakistani agents might infiltrate into India as refugees and stir up communal strife. But apart from these no doubt weighty considerations a protracted struggle in East Bengali is not necessarily to India's disadvantage. The longer the conflict lasts the greater in the long run will be the cost to Pakistan and the greater the emasculation of its power. From Pakistan's point of view, economic, military and also political constraints dictate that they must avoid becoming bogged down in an indecisive and protracted war.

In sum, therefore, whatever the outcome of the current conflict in East Bengal, Pakistan's overall national power will be significantly reduced, and its ability to act as a countervailing balance against India, which was doubtful, will lose all credibility.

Pakistan will, however, stand to gain a lot if it succeeds even temporarily in suppressing the freedom movement. China's influence with it will grow immensely in that event, and other major powers may decide to compete with China and each other in giving military and economic aid for rebuilding Pakistani power, even though it remains unlikely that it will ever be restored to its former level. As things now stand, therefore, India's interests are better served by East Bengal winning independence or at least a substantial degree of autonomy. In deciding what steps should be taken to give effect to India's proclaimed sympathy and support for the East Bengal liberation struggle, all the likely benefits and costs of the various options must be pragmatically and accurately evaluated.

PLANNING FOR DISPARITY*

DR. ARJUN SENGUPTA

AROUND THE middle of 1960s, international opinion, particularly in the west, was passing through an euphoria about the economic performance of Pakistan. *New York Times* wrote on January 18, 1965: "Pakistan may be on its way towards an economic milestone that so far has been reached by only

* The statistics and other information about the economy of Pakistan used in this paper are taken from the following sources:
1. *The Fourth Five Year Plan, 1970-75*, Planning Commission, Pakistan;
2. *Pakistan Economic Survey*, 1969-70;
3. *Statistical Bulletin* (monthly, CSO Pakistan);
4. *East Pakistan*, 1968;
5. *Pakistan Year Book*, 1970;
6. Stephen R. Louis: *Pakistan: Industrialisation and Trade Policies*, OECD, Paris;
7. Mahubub-Ul-Haq; *The Strategy of Economic Planning*; for Oxford University Press;
8. G. Pappanek; *Pakistan Development, Social Goals and Private Incentives*, Harvard;
9. An article called "East-West Pakistan; a Problem in the Political Economy of Planning"; by Prof. Anisur Rahaman.

The author has most heavily drawn on Prof. Rahaman's brilliant article.

one other populous country, the United States". This comment is representative of a wide cross-section of the opinions
expressed in the press and at professional meetings of economists
in the United States and Great Britain. They were based on
the performance of Pakistan during its Second Plan period,
1959-60 to 1964-65. The gross national product of Pakistan
grew only at the rate of 2.6 per cent between 1949-50 and 1954-
55, hardly keeping pace with the growth of population. During
the First Plan period, 1954-55 and 1959-60, the growth rate
was reduced to 2.4 per cent, with no increase whatsoever in
per capita income. But suddenly, in the Second Plan period,
the GNP showed a rate of growth of about 5.3 per cent, raising
the rate of growth of per capita income to 2.7 per cent.

This sharp break was considered to be a clear signal that a
new era had dawned on Pakistan. A military regime had taken
over the administration of Pakistan just a year before the
Second Plan period began. Whatever might have been its im-
plication for freedom and democracy, the change did usher in
a period of stability in the government and its administration,
foreign policy and approach to economic planning. Stability
became the key word in describing the polity of Pakistan, and
it was obviously much more highly regarded by western opinion
than democracy, popular representation or freedom in this part
of backward Asia.

For an economist, five years of experience would be a fragile
base under any circumstances for developing any grand hypo-
thesis about the performance of an economy. Several things,
it is true, did happen in Pakistan. There were signs that
agriculture in West Pakistan was almost on the threshold of a
potential revolution. The industrial structure was moving away
from the production of light consumer goods in the Second
Plan period, and industries producing investment and related
goods grew at a rate almost double that of the consumer goods
industries and 70 per cent higher than industries producing
intermediate goods. There was a marked liberalisation of import
policy and a very steep increase in foreign aid. The total
foreign assistance to Pakistan during the First Plan was only
about $ 964 million. During the Second Plan period it was
as much as $ 2,351 million. There were also some observable
changes in economic policy favourable to growth. But still,
five years is too small a period to offer any firm conclusions

about the course of the economy of a country, especially a country like Pakistan which has problems unique to itself and much more difficult to analyse than most of the other less developed countries.

Very few economists who recommended the example of Pakistan to other poor countries realised that something was happening underneath the statistics of aggregate growth and prosperity which would literally explode and only five years after the end of the Second Plan period would practically break the whole system apart.

From the beginning, Pakistan was a country with two distinct economies. East and West Pakistan were different in almost every relevant sense and separated by more than a thousand miles of hostile territory. It would take a common man at least 10 days to travel one way between the two wings; he would have to travel by ship from one extreme of the Bay of Bengal to the opposite extreme of the Arabian Sea. Anyone migrating from one region to the other in search of a job would have to carry with him provisions for at least a month, and the total cost would be almost equal to the annual per capita income of the country. There has always been a very severe shortage of shipping space in Pakistan and many restrictions on the movement of merchandise, both foreign and domestic, from one region to another. This shortage and the cost of sea transport alone was sufficient to keep the country split into two economies. Prosperity in one region could not be shared by people migrating from the other region, nor could goods of the richer western region be sold to the poorer eastern region except at a much higher cost. It should have been obvious that the only way to keep Pakistan as a viable union of these two regions was to develop both of them at more or less the same pace. The history of Pakistan is a clear record of failure to perceive this elementary notion of political economy.

Throughout the period 1949-50 to 1964-65 the gross provincial product grew at a rate of 2.8 per cent in East Pakistan but at 4 per cent in West Pakistan. The provincial product per capita showed virtually no rise in East Pakistan but a growth of about 15 per cent in West Pakistan. Agriculture grew at a rate of 1.7 per cent per year in East Pakistan while the non-agricultural economy grew at 4.6 per cent a year. The corresponding rates for West Pakistan are 2.5 and 5.5 per cent a year.

The picture was more miserable before 1959-60. East Pakistan's regional income grew at a rate of only 1.4 per cent a year during the 10 year period 1949-50 to 1959-60. Per capita income actually declined during this whole period. West Pakistan's growth was not particularly impressive, but still it was 3.5 per cent a year, more than double the rate of growth in East Pakistan, and the per capita income grew at the rate of 1.1 per cent. There was virtually no growth in agriculture in East Pakistan in this period, whereas West Pakistan showed a slow but perceptible growth of 2 per cent a year.

The growth rates in the two regions were much closer to each other in the Second Plan period although still higher in West than in East Pakistan. But this did not really alter the picture, for to counter what was done during the 10 years between 1949 and 1959 a much higher rate of growth should have been planned in East Pakistan than in West. It is true that both in the First and Second Plan documents there were signs of awareness of the difficulties of unequal regional development but neither really went to the root of the matter. The First Plan document observed: "The problem of regional development is specially acute between East and West Pakistan because they are more than a thousand miles apart. There is little movement of population between the two wings. Even the movement of goods cannot be as free and smooth as in contiguous areas. This means that so far as possible and subject to the other objectives of the programme, economic opportunities should be moved to the people rather than people to the opportunities." But when it came to allocating funds to the two regions, West Pakistan was given Rs. 535 crores in the original plan and Rs. 406 crores in the revised plan as against Rs. 400 crores for East Pakistan in the original plan and Rs. 352 crores in the revised plan. The actual performance was substantially different. The public sector spent Rs. 594 crores in West Pakistan as against only Rs. 332 crores in East Pakistan during the First Plan. No breakdown was given for the actual or anticipated private investment.

During the Second Plan also the public sector allocation was heavily biased in favour of West Pakistan. In the first version of the Second Plan, the proposed expenditure was Rs. 1,900 crores, of which Rs. 1,300 crores was to be spent in the public sector and Rs. 600 crores in the private sector. About 45 per cent of the public sector funds were to be spent in East Pakistan. Subsequently, the plan was revised, raising the size to Rs. 2,300 crores, with Rs. 1,462 crores for the public sector and Rs. 838 crores for the private sector. The allocation to East Pakistan out of the total public sector outlay was around 44 per cent. There was further provision of Rs. 518 crores for the Indus Basin Replacement project and works programme, but as before this was kept outside the plan outlay. The actual outlay in the public sector during the Second Plan was about Rs. 1,395 crores, nearly 50 per cent short of what was proposed, and the allocation to East Pakistan out of this reduced total remained around 44 per cent as proposed in the Plan. But the private sector investment during the Second Plan went upto Rs. 1,368 crores—about 63 per cent higher than the sum originally provided. Estimates of the regional breakdown of these private investments are not very firm, but the official documents mention that East Pakistan received only about a third.

It is difficult to explain why higher investment of development expenditure was not provided for East Pakistan to help it achieve a higher growth rate. The First Plan document denied that there was "any significant difference in the magnitude of potential economic opportunities in the two wings." The Second Plan gave a woolly explanation for its original allocation—"that it was guided by the need" to maximise development in the less developed parts of the country without prejudicing national development as a whole. It is woolly because it does not examine with any degree of precision the implicit assumption that a higher allocation to East Pakistan would reduce the rate of national development.

Mehbubul Haq, one of the architects of Pakistan's economic policy during the Ayub regime, wrote in 1963, that is in the middle of the period of the Second Plan, "It is difficult to make any assessment of the relative growth potential of East and West Pakistan, but at least there is nothing to suggest that the difference is a significant one." But the figures of the rate of savings and capital output ratios in the two regions provided by Haq himself show that the Second Plan objective of maximising the development of the poorer region without reducing the overall national growth would have called for a much higher allocation in favour of East Pakistan. The rate of gross domestic saving as given by Haq during the First Plan period was 6.5 per cent in East Pakistan compared to 5.3 per cent in West Pakistan. On the other hand the capital output ratio in East was only 1.4 compared to 2.3 in West Pakistan. If these figures are correct then the planners should have seen that the productivity of scarce capital was higher in East than in West Pakistan. As the savings generated out of income were also higher in East Pakistan, each rupee of investment diverted from West Pakistan to East would have increased not only the growth of the poorer region but also the rate of development of the nation as a whole.

One would not put much faith in this kind of aggregate analysis for planning in a complex economy, but there is no indication at least from the reading of the Second Plan that a very sophisticated exercise went into its formulation. In any case none is reflected in the explanations provided for the allocation of funds.

Analysis was much more sophisticated in the formulation of the Third Plan, and it was in this that for the first time allocations for East Pakistan appeared to be higher than for West Pakistan. It allocated 53 per cent of public sector outlays to East Pakistan and 47 per cent to West Pakistan. But in the first place, the actual expenditure fell short of the target of Rs. 3,000 crores by 27 per cent. In the second place expenditure on the Indus Basin replacement works, located entirely in West Pakistan, was again regarded as outside the plan and so was not included in the figures of public sector outlays! It was also in this plan that for the first time the total private sector investment was divided half and half between the two regions, that is Rs. 1,100 crores for each wing. But the actual achievement here went totally astray. Private investment in East Pakistan, as estimated in 1969-70, would be Rs. 544 crores for the entire Third Plan and only about a third of the private investment in West Pakistan, which was expected to be Rs. 1,620 crores.

It is clear that the factors responsible for the disparity between the two wings of Pakistan are too fundamental to be wished away or juggled out of existence by tinkering with expected plan outlays. If one wants to reduce the parity there is no other means except planned development. But as I said in the beginning there has been practically no searching study or analysis of the causes of the disparity, and that is the prerequisite for any attempt to reduce it. In the absence of such a study the awareness of the hardships of the poorer region and the pious intention to do something to remove the disparity which is reflected in the official documents of Pakistan cannot but remain ineffective.

The fact of the disparity was so obvious even in the middle 'sixties that it should have struck at least some fear in the minds of planners if they were genuinely interested in keeping Pakistan as a viable union. Before 1954-55 the per capita income was 15 per cent higher in West Pakistan than in East Pakistan. During the First Plan period it became about 32 per cent higher and in the Second Plan—the plan which was so universally acclaimed as a great success—it was more than 30 per cent higher! And this rising graph of disparity really understates its magnitude. There were substantial differences between the two wings in the prices of almost all commodities, and since, and most especially, the prices of items of mass consumption were higher in the East, the purchasing power of a rupee was much lower in East Pakistan than in West. As Mehbubul Haq points out, in 1959-60 a ton of rice cost more than twice as much in East Pakistan as a ton of wheat in West Pakistan. "This means that even if an average East Pakistani is getting the same nutrition from his rice diet as an average West Pakistani from his wheat diet, he is accredited with more income because rice is an expensive crop in national income accounting terms." If corrections were made for this single item of consumption, Haq observes, then the true extent of the disparity in per capita income between West and East Pakistan in 1959-60 would be almost double that of what is shown in the statistics.

There has not been much difference in the per capita consumption of foodgrains between the two regions in physical terms, but as mentioned, an average East Pakistani had to pay more for his food. It is important to note this fact because the per capita foodgrains consumption in both wings of Pakistan is barely sufficient to meet the immediate subsistence requirements. If an East Pakistani had to spend about double the amount of money on foodgrains compared to an average West Pakistani just in order to subsist, he was left with a very much smaller proportion out of a much smaller income to spend on other commodities.

If adjustments were made for differences in the prices of some other consumer goods, the real income disparity would be seen to be even larger and if we look into the per capita consumption of a few selected commodities the nature of the disparity becomes even more clear. Between 1951-52 and 1959-60 the average per capita consumption of refined sugar was 2.7 lbs in East Pakistan compared to 6.8 lbs in West Pakistan. The corresponding figures for raw sugar were 16.1 lbs and 46.9 lbs, for tea 0.1 lb and 0.8 lbs, for cloth 2.2 yards and 7.8 yards, for cigarettes 21 pieces and 121. For luxury commodities like motor cars the West Pakistan consumption was nine times as large as in East, and for radios seven times as large. Some of the figures of per capita consumption in 1969-70 are: pulses, excluding gram, 6.7 lbs for East Pakistan, 8.0 for West; fats and oils 6.4 lbs and 14 lbs, for milk 21 lbs and 228 lbs, for refined sugar 5.6 lbs and 15.89 lbs; and for cotton cloth 10.8 yards and 13.2 yards.

Equally important in terms of its explosive content is the further fact brought out in a recent study, that while the average East Pakistani was much poorer than the average West Pakistani, the distribution of income within East Pakistan was such that it was pushing more and more people in the eastern region below the poverty line. The disparity between the rural poor in East Pakistan and the rich in West Pakistan was rising at a faster rate than the disparity between average income in the two regions.

One can go on giving similar figures from many different branches of economic life to portray the staggering nature of the economic disparity between the two regions. Per capita income and consumption disparities are just the reflections of severe differences in the rates of growth in almost all sectors of the economy, such as agriculture, manufacturing, transport, trade, housing, services, banking and insurance. In most sectors there was evidence of a distinct trend towards a further widening of the disparity over the entire period of planning. In some other sectors, no trend could be established but there was almost no sector in which there was the opposite trend.

The facts of this disparity are easy to identify, but it is not easy to formulate the causes. Very little work has been done in this field. But still one has to tackle this problem if one wishes to make even a beginning towards understanding the nature of the present crisis in Pakistan. In the short span of this section I wish to offer some tentative hypotheses. They are naturally very rough and general and without further examination should not be taken as firmly proved.

When Pakistan was created there was nothing in the nature of its economy which could indicate that West Pakistan would tend to grow at a much faster rate than East Pakistan or that the difference between the per capita incomes of the two regions would grow so much. At the time of the partition both the wings were primarily agricultural: West producing cotton and wheat and East, jute and rice. There was very little industry in either. There was not much difference in the infrastructure of the two wings; the availability of power was insignificant, the value added by transport and communication was slightly higher in East Pakistan than in West, whereas in trade, finance and services West Pakistan had an edge over East.

And yet within the next ten years the production structure in West Pakistan was altered sufficiently to generate a high rate of growth in comparison with East Pakistan. The major cause of this process was official economic policy. In the initial period official economic policy was only marginally concerned with agriculture. There was some allocation in favour of agriculture in the plan programmes but they did not reveal any very specific purpose. The main orientation of policy was towards industrialisation. Immediately after the partition, Pakistan had a very wide market for all kinds of manufactures which were almost wholly imported either from India or from other countries. With the banning of most of the imports, Pakistan's industries were gifted with a wide and protected field of operation. There was a short-lived Korean war boom between 1950 and 1952, after which, with a fall in export prices, the government introduced severe import controls, which continued until about the beginning of the Second Plan. The largest protection was received by consumer goods manufacturers as the import of these items was completely prohibited.

Side by side with this, Pakistan refused to devalue its rupee until 1955, which made it difficult for the country to expand its exports. Since Pakistan's exports were predominantly agricultural commodities, this meant a squeeze on agricultural income. On the other hand, import of investment goods like machinery, equipment and raw materials was allowed at the official exchange rate, and since the domestic currency was highly over-valued, this meant a large subsidy for manufacturers. It was expected that in the circumstances the manufacture of consumer goods, which was based mostly on domestically produced raw materials, would grow at a very rapid rate in both wings of Pakistan. Statistics show that the manufacture of consumption goods grew at 43 per cent a year between 1951-52 and 1954-55, at about 15.6 per cent a year between 1954-55 and 1959-60 and at 13.3 per cent between 1959-60 and and 1964-65. The initial year's figures were abnormally high because of the low base at the start, but still the rate of growth was significantly large throughout the period. But even in this sector, industries were turning up much more rapidly in West Pakistan than in East. East Pakistan's major industries which grew over this period were jute, textile, tea manufacturing, safety matches and some paper goods. Of these, jute textiles were the major industry. In West Pakistan on the other hand phenomenal growth occurred in the cotton textile industry during this period, as well as in tobacco manufacturing, sugar, silk textiles, edible oil, footwear and paper board.

Although imports were more liberal for intermediate and investment goods, the domestic demand for them was growing very rapidly and soon, from around the mid-fifties, industries producing these goods started emerging in Pakistan and growing at a very rapid rate. But very little of this investment went to East Pakistan. This could not be explained in terms of the availability of domestic raw materials and knowhow because they were not available in West Pakistan either and were almost wholly imported. Yet by 1959-60 West Pakistan had an industrial base producing basic metals and metal products, transport equipment, chemicals and pharmaceuticals, machinery and equipment and several other miscellaneous items.

How does one explain the difference in industrial development in the two regions? Official plan documents try to rationalise it mainly in terms of the relative availability of skills and technical proficiencies, but they are unconvincing. Technical skills do not grow out of nothing. They depend on training and educational facilities and on learning by doing. It is true that over time, West Pakistan acquired a large stock of engineers and technical personnel; enrolment in engineering, industrial and secondary technical institutions in 1958 was 6,068 in West Pakistan and only 2,384 in East Pakistan. But this difference implies discrimination against East Pakistan. The literacy rate in East Pakistan is higher than in West and it could have trained technical personnel just as well if it had been given the technical institutions and enrolment facilities which were given to West Pakistan. The other training process, learning by doing, would have worked just as well wherever industry was located.

A more basic fact is that most of the knowhow for industrialisation was actually imported, just as most of the raw material was. In other words the major explanation for the unequal industrial growth in the two wings lies in the difference in their capacity to import, and it is here that a mechanism was set up in Pakistan which can legitimately be described as a process of systematic exploitation of East by West Pakistan.

Till about 1959-60 the amount of foreign aid flowing to Pakistan was very small compared to its export earnings, and most of these earnings were provided by East Pakistan throughout this period. During the period 1950-51 and 1954-55, East Pakistan accounted for more than 50 per cent of the total export earnings of Pakistan; for the period 1955-56 to 1959-60 it provided for more than 61 per cent. On the other hand East Pakistan's share in the total imports of the country throughout the period 1950-51 to 1959-60 was less than 30 per cent. This meant that throughout this period East Pakistan had a net export surplus with the outside world and West Pakistan a net import surplus. In simple words this means that substantial foreign exchange earnings of East Pakistan were being diverted to West Pakistan.

East Pakistan consistently had a deficit in its trade with West Pakistan, implying that it was buying more from than it was selling to West Pakistan. This fact is quoted by West Pakistan spokesmen as evidence of the transfer of West Pakistan's resources to East Pakistan during this period. Even if West Pakistan's export surplus to East Pakistan is taken at its face value, it does not compensate for the loss of resources incurred by East Pakistan through its surplus account in international trade. During the period 1950-51 and 1954-55, East Pakistan was losing on an average Rs. 26.2 crores a year. During the First Plan period, 1955-56 to 1959-60, it was losing Rs. 7.1 crores a year. And all this in nominal value; the true measure of loss of resources by East Pakistan is much higher. First of all, Pakistan's currency was over-valued by very much more than 50 per cent over this whole period. West Pakistan goods were sold in East Pakistan at a much higher price than in West Pakistan, and in many cases the price was substantially greater than the usual transport cost would justify. This means that each dollar of foreign exchange earned by East Pakistan and transferred to West, bought for West Pakistan much more than the official rupee equivalent to a dollar would have bought.

It would therefore not be unreasonable to double the nominal value of the export surplus of East Pakistan in international trade and deduct from that the value of its deficit with West Pakistan in the internal trade to get an indication of the resources drained away from East Pakistan during this period. By that calculation, during the pre-plan period between 1950-51 and 1954-55, East Pakistan was losing about Rs. 97 crores a year and during the First Plan period, between 1955-56 and 1959-60, about Rs. 34 crores a year. This entire sum was available to West Pakistan to increase its domestic supply of resources. Indeed on foreign trade account alone West Pakistan was running a deficit, at the official exchange rate of Rs. 20 crores a year during the pre-plan period, and Rs. 91 crores a year during the First Plan period. This substantial amount of import surplus allowed West Pakistan to develop the command over resources needed for domestic industrial development which was mentioned above as the principal factor explaining its high rate of growth relative to East Pakistan.

Whatever foreign capital inflow was taking place before the Second Plan was not equitably distributed between the two wings. If one splits the total foreign aid received by Pakistan by weightage according to population between the two regions, as one legitimately should, the figures for transfer of resources from East Pakistan would increase very substantially. In any case since upto 1959-60 East Pakistan's overall balance of trade showed a surplus, it means there was no net inflow of foreign aid resources into that region. Any imports financed by foreign aid which flowed into East Pakistan were more than off-set by the export of goods from East to West. During the Second Plan period East Pakistan continued to have a surplus on foreign trade account of about Rs. 4 crores a year. Since the deficit on account of trade with West Pakistan averaged Rs. 42

crores a year during this period, there was, for the first time, a net inflow of resources of the order of Rs. 38 crores per annum into East Pakistan. But during the same period West Pakistan's deficit on foreign trade account was Rs. 192 crores a year, more than double the average deficit during the First Plan period. If one deducts the surplus of West Pakistan on internal trade account, this region received about Rs. 149 crores a year as a net inflow of resources during the Second Plan period.

The picture that emerges from all these facts is that East Pakistan was consistently the main earner of foreign exchange for the whole of the country throughout the planning period. Whatever East Pakistani exporters got in foreign exchange they had to surrender to the Central Government against rupee funds, and that too at a rate of exchange which was substantially over-valued in favour of the rupee. The foreign exchange earned by East and West Pakistan, plus the inflow of foreign aid, formed the central pool of external resources for the whole country, but it was very unequally divided between the two regions.

Throughout the period West Pakistan's total imports were between 120 to 140 per cent higher than the imports of East Pakistan. With its foreign exchange earnings, after deducting its very small share of imports from other countries, East Pakistan had to purchase goods from West Pakistan which were much more expensive than in the world market. It has been pointed out that if raw cotton had been freely allowed to be imported from West Pakistan to be processed in East, the cost of cotton textiles in East Pakistan would have been lower than the cost of textiles imported from West Pakistan, and East Pakistan would have had a textile industry to boot.

It is not necessary to find a deliberate policy by the Government of Pakistan to exploit the East in favour of the West. Inability or unwillingness to reverse the trend would be sufficient to prove the continuous and large transfer of resources from East to West Pakistan. In so far as the official policy of industrialisation discriminated against agriculture, there was a general discrimination against the eastern wing, which is overwhelmingly agricultural. Second, the government's policy of import licensing, biased in favour of established importers who were mostly in West Pakistan, resulted in a large concentration of licences in West Pakistan, especially in the hands of migrants from India who were traditionally engaged in trade.

With the gradual tightening of the import controls and with the increasing profitability of consumer goods industries—ranging between 50 per cent and 100 per cent—most of these traders converted themselves into industrialists and started their factories in and around Karachi. Not until 1970, when open general licensing was introduced, was the dominant position of the established importers broken or enterpreneurship given a fair chance to develop in East Pakistan.

Till around the middle 'sixties, commercial licences were the principal type of import licences given in Pakistan. These imports were locally resaleable, and they commanded prices in the domestic market which were much higher than world prices. In 1959, 95 per cent of raw materials for capital goods, 44 per cent of raw materials for consumer goods and 28 per cent of capital goods imported were covered by commercial licences. This was at a time when the relative importance of commercial business in the total number of issued licences had sharply declined, compared to the early 'fifties. In 1959-60, Karachi alone received 42 per cent to 48 per cent of all the commercial licences issued. The whole of West Pakistan, including Karachi, received 60 per cent to 68 per cent and the whole of East Pakistan between 32 per cent and 40 per cent. These figures are fairly representative of the entire period. Of the industrial import licences, the other principal source of imports, in 1959-60 East Pakistan's share was very similar, between 31 to 40 per cent and for Karachi alone between 36 and 38 per cent.

It is true that in general the rule of the thumb was used in granting licences, and such rules generally favour the established practice. But it is also true that whatever discretionary power the controlling authorities had was rarely used in favour of East Pakistan. Prof. Anisur Rehman has talked about a commodity called economic patronage, which summarises all the special favours that the bureaucracy in a tightly controlled regime can confer on the people. The bureaucracy in Pakistan was overwhelmingly West Pakistani. In 1960, none of the 16 Secretaries to the Government, and only one of the 36 Joint Secretaries, was from East Pakistan. Out of a total of 2,779 first class officers in the various central services in 1960, 87 per cent were West Pakistanis. These people were really the government in practice; they decided the policies about loans, grants, subsidies, taxation, tarriffs and licences. Add to this the fact that the capital of Pakistan has all along been in the western wing of the country. "In such an economy", as Prof. Rehman says "it is easy to see the distinct advantages conferred on a region due to its nearness to the authorities concerned with these functions. Apart from the greater ease and economy of communication, there are intangible but obvious advantages of a closer contact with the authorities. All administrators are human beings and some are susceptible to pecuniary incentives. That direct controls and corruption tend to go together is widely recognised. The tendency would be the greater, the greater the margin of the scarcity price of the administrative service in question over what is laid down as its official price (for example, the rate of interest of centrally administered loans, the price of foreign exchange, the fees for licences). This is really nothing but the application of economic analysis to a special case of monopolistic supply facing competitive demand. The commodity in question may be called for convenience 'economic patronage', a term already in vogue in the country. In view of the policy of licensing regulations and controls over key economic resources, like capital and foreign exchange, exercised by the central authorities, 'economic patronage' must be regarded as an essential scarce input for most economic undertakings in Pakistan."

So far we have tried to give a general picture of the process of unequal regional development in Pakistan. The civil war, which erupted recently is a logical culmination of that process, leading to a total split of the country into two independent economies. Although officially the independence of Bangla Desh was declared only at the end of March this year, its economy was functioning independently between March 1 and March 25, virtually under the control of the leadership of Mujibur Rehman. The major economic plank of the independence movement, which until March 26 was really a movement for greater regional autonomy, was control over foreign exchange resources, the region's own trading activities, the investment of resources and instruments for mobilising them. It is not possible to say what would have been the nature of the experiment if regional autonomy with all its implications had been actually given a chance, but now that is a closed chapter. Anyone writing on the economy of Bangla Desh today has to talk of the prospects of Bangla Desh for survival in separation from West Pakistan and for eventually developing a viable and prosperous economy.

It is difficult to talk of either of these two problems—the problem of survival in the immediate future and of viability and growth potential in the long run—without a knowledge of what remains of East Pakistan's stock of resources in terms of capital goods, installed machinery and equipment, factories, dams, bridges, buildings and, most important, manpower after the ravaging war with West Pakistan is over. If Bangla Desh did not have to start totally afresh, its potential for growing into a viable and eventually prosperous economy would have been substantial. Its jute would have continued to earn large amounts of foreign exchange. In 1968-69, exports of raw jute and jute manufactures contributed about 40 per cent to the total export earnings of the whole of Pakistan. With a litle better planning, production and export of raw jute could have been expanded at a much faster rate than so far. The area under jute is highly susceptible to adverse relative price with rice which had been showing a rising trend. In addition, the price the growers receive depends very much upon the organisation of marketing and standardisation and proper sampling of varieties.

Pakistan had also followed a policy of diverting as much raw jute as possible to local manufacturers, though costs of production were rather high. The jute industry expanded quite rapidly and maintained a competitive position with Indian exports through substantial subsidies. Even if Bangla Desh does not come to any understanding with India, it should be able to maintain its export earnings. But cooperation with India should reduce its domestic cost and also raise the value of exports of raw jute and jute goods through a coordination of production and trade on the basis of comparative advantage.

In the early sixties, besides jute, fish, tea and hides and skins were the major export items of East Bengal. Around 1961-62 or 1962-63, they were contributing about 5 per cent to 6 per cent of Pakistan's total export earnings. Their export outlets gradually dried up by the end of the sixties. The decline of the fish trade was entirely due to the decline in trade with India. Raw hides and skins were diverted to the internal tanning industry and domestic consumption, and by 1966-67, tanned or dressed hides and skins and leather manufactures emerged as an export item worth more than Rs. 5 crores. The disappearance of tea from the export trade was mainly because of diversion to the West Pakistan market. Because of the nature of the production process its extension could not be dramatic, but still the production of tea rose from about 51 million lbs in 1959-60 to about 67 million lbs in 1966-67. In the second half of the fifties the value of the exports was around Rs. 3 crores to 4 crores. But by 1966-67 it was only about Rs. 8 lakhs. During the same period there was a remarkable rise in tea exports from East to West. In 1960-61, the value was Rs. 10.9 crores but in 1966-67 it was as much as Rs. 29 crores. So, this could again emerge as an export earner.

It is important to remember that throughout the planning period, except for three or four years, East Pakistan's exports were significantly higher than its imports in foreign exchange. In recent years, the gap has become narrower because of a decline in the world price of jute and rice in development imports. East Pakistan had a deficit in the inter-wing trade with West Pakistan, which tended to grow over time. But with the closure of this trade, a substantial part of the exports to West Pakistan can be diverted to the world market, since they are very similar to the commodities currently exported to the outside world. The total export earnings of Bangla Desh then would not fall very short of its import requirements even at the level of pre-liberation war economic activities.

The inputs from West Pakistan were in any case much more costly than in the world market. The manufactured goods imported from West Pakistan, like cotton fabrics, machinery, drugs and medicines, tobacco manufacture and cement could easily be imported immediately from substitute sources and eventually produced domestically. But there would remain, for quite a few years, an absolute shortage of some of the major primary commodities which were up to now imported from West Pakistan, like raw cotton, oil seeds, tobacco and foodgrains. Bangla Desh would have to search for the cheapest source for these products, which would not be India.

Several natural gas desposits which have been discovered in East Bengal have already been put to use for industrial purposes, including manufacture of fertilizers. The paper industry, which became quite substantial in the middle sixties, has the poten-

tial for growing much larger, and in Chittagong a beginning has been made with the production of steel. Several
other industries like cotton textiles, sugar, cigarettes, tyres
and tubes and cement are already in operation and their performance in terms of efficiency has not been very different
from that in West Pakistan. East Bengal is the main source
of matches for the whole of the country. In metals and metal
products, machinery and equipment very little capacity has
been created in East Bengal till now. Since they are overwhelmingly based on imported raw materials, there is no reason
why these industries cannot grow as rapidly and efficiently, if
not more, as in West Pakistan.

But the main problem is that of survival. Rice is the
principal foodgrain in East Bengal, and during the floods last
November a lot of damage was done to standing crops. The
total consumption of rice in East Bengal in 1968-69 was of
the order of 11.4 million tons. In 1969-70 it was about three
lakh tons higher than the domestic production. Last year the
production must have been lower and even the government
planned to import 4.65 lakh tons. If this is regarded as the
order of the deficit before the civil war started, it must be
much higher now. The Fourth Plan document shows that
per capita consumption of pulses, fats and oils, vegetables,
fish and meat, milk, fruits, sugar and several other commodities
in East Bengal was much lower than the minimum required
according to nutritional standards. The war would have defi-
nitely reduced the consumption of these items even further.

In order to give some rough estimates of the total amounts
of different essential commodities that Bangla Desh would
require now to survive in the immediate future, we should
make the general assumption that for 1970-71 only half of the
total amount produced in 1969-70 would be available for
domestic consumption. This figure should not be wide off
the mark. All indications show that the level of production in
1970-71 was not much different from that in 1969-70.
Besides, as for most commodities consumption lags behind
production by about six months to a year and some agricultural production, although disrupted, would still continue.
The total demand for these commodities in 1970-71 is taken
to be of the same order as in 1969-70. It should be higher if for
nothing else than the rise in population but for a rough idea

one might accept the total demand in the current year to be the same as last year. The deficit in rice on this assumption turns out to be more than five lakh tons, but the deficit in wheat turns out to be more than a million tons. It should be noted that though East Bengal has been predominantly a rice eating country, over time it has met a large part of the deficit in food by consuming wheat, mostly imported from West Pakistan. In 1969-70 the total consumption of wheat in East Bengal was one million seventy thousand tons, whereas the domestic production was only 75 thousand tons. If only half of the total domestic output of wheat of that year is available now, there is a deficit of a million and thirty thousand tons. Since one does not see any chance of this wheat coming from West Pakistan, if alternative sources of supply cannot be found the requirement of the rice in Bangla Desh would be much higher than five lakh tons. On the other hand the rice requirement can be reduced if wheat can be procured.

For pulses, the deficit would be about 96 thousand tons, and for vegetables, including potatoes, more than a million tons. The shortfall in white sugar would also be of the order of one lakh tons. This requirement could be reduced by using a lower quality of sugar and gur, particularly since sugarcane production in Bangla Desh is not too much. For edible oil, Bangla Desh has a major problem. Mustard oil is its principal cooking medium and the domestic resources are very inadequate. The estimate of production given in the Fourth Plan document is of the order of 170,000 tons in 1969-70. If one considers that some amount of cottage industry scale production continues and if one also takes into account the normal import, reasonable estimate of the requirement would be 150,000 tons.

In cotton cloth the deficit is exceptionally large. On the basis of per capita consumption of 10.9 yards the total demand was estimated in 1969-70 to be of the order of 786 million yards. Of this the domestic production accounted for hardly 60 million yards. If one considers that in the critical period after the war one would not expect more than five yards of consumption per capita, the minimum import requirement would be 350 million yards since most of the cotton mills would be out of production. The other major items of deficit in Bangla Desh are salt, kerosene and coal. It does not produce any significant amount of salt and used to import most of its needs from West Pakistan. The same is true for kerosene and coal; imports have been the main source of supply.

In an overall view, it would seem that Bangla Desh would not face insuperable problems either for its survival in the short-term or for future growth once survival has been ensured, as it can be, with the help of friendly countries as well as—or even more—through extremely careful and rigorous internal economic management. It will, of course, face acute hardships in the meantime, and some problems will be especially tricky, as for example that of floating its own currency, which the Bangla Desh Government appears to be anxious to do; the transition from the present Pakistani currency to the proposed new one would call for very skillful fiscal management, especially during the transitional period when both currencies would be in use. These problems would be difficult enough to face if West Pakistan did not needlessly prolong this mutually ruinous and tragic war. If Islamabad decided to facilitate it, the transition from East Pakistan to Bangla Desh would be much less painful for East Bengal, but it would be not only painful but ruinous if West Pakistan decided to make it so out of blindness, viciousness or sheer obstinacy.

But the position is not very different for West Pakistan either. Its own recovery from the present disaster depends almost entirely upon how and how soon the civil war is ended. If Islamabad won back a cooperative and friendly East Pakistan, though that seems to be the least likely of all possibilities now, by offering a political settlement acceptable to the broad mass of the people of East Bengal, both wings could hope to recover from the nearly fatal wounds which both have suffered; friendly assistance would then be available to both in significant if not entirely adequate measure. Or if West Pakistan realised that a prolonged war would only delay, not prevent, the break away of the eastern wing, and decided to shorten the agony of the separation by accepting it as the nearly inevitable consequence of its own past policies, it could hope to get to a course of recovery a few years hence. It would be an agonising recovery, but not an impossible one; in return for willingness to call off the bloodshed which has been condemned all over the world, West Pakistan could hope for assistance on the magnitude which it needs for its survival and future economic stability. But if it preferred only to try to grind the Bangla

Desh people into the ground in a fit of self-destructive madness, its own ruination, perhaps economic before political, would be as inevitable as that of Bangla Desh.

The actual military cost of running this war with Bangla Desh may or may not be very substantial. I am not competent to judge the accuracy of the figure of Rs. 1 crore as given by some experts, but in terms of the burden on the economy, with an additional defence expenditure of even Rs. 100 crores to Rs. 150 crores plus the cost of the administration in occupying Bangla Desh must be quite substantial for an economy whose resource base has already shrunk. The alternative scenarios are therefore the same for West Pakistan as they are for East Bengal—a difficult but possible recovery if the war is replaced by an agreement one way or another and an international assistance programme is begun on a large scale; otherwise a rapid decline towards disintegration which may soon become irreversible and lead to consequences which are difficult to foresee but are bound to be on a scale bigger than anyone is facing at present.

As I mentioned earlier, West Pakistan was exporting a substantial amount of its output to East Bengal over the last two decades of planning. In fact the magnitude of this trade increased quite substantially during the Third Five Year Plan period. While it was exporting about Rs. 56 crores worth of goods per year to East Bengal during the First Plan period and Rs. 88 crores a year during the Second Plan, in the Third Plan period the figure went up to Rs. 120 crores a year. This is quite close to the figure of West Pakistan's total exports to other countries. So the loss of the East Bengal market will have quite a substantial impact on the production system in West Pakistan. The commodities which West Pakistan imported from East are mostly tea, jute goods, paper, matches, leather and some other small items. Their loss would have some impact on West Pakistan's economy. But except for jute goods and paper—and tea, which West Pakistanis might have to do without for a few years—the loss of these imports would not create an insurmountable problem. But the problems resulting from the loss of the East Bengal market would be very great.

Of the major manufactures exported from West to East, cotton textiles accounted for Rs. 27.8 crores in 1968-69 as against Rs. 30.8 crores worth to the rest of the world. Since most of the cotton textile exports of Pakistan are from West Pakistan, it is clear that the value of the exports to East Bengal was almost equal to the value of the exports to the rest of the world. This offers a very difficult problem to West Pakistan. Not only is the cotton textile industry the largest industry in West Pakistan, it is also quite inefficient in terms of world prices. Besides, the prices at which these goods were sold in East Bengal were much higher than those obtainable in other countries. To remove the glut in this industry would require a substantial squeeze in profits, whether the textiles are sold in the domestic market or abroad. The immediate result would be some increase in unemployment and consequent labour trouble. In a military regime such difficulties may be more easily contained than in a democracy, but signs of discontent have already come out into the open. The exports of other commodities to East Bengal were also not an insignificant proportion of the total value added in those industries in West Pakistan. They too will shrink with the loss of the East Bengal market, resulting in a further economic decline and sharper unemployment in West Pakistan.

But if West Pakistan accepts the separation of Bangla Desh instead of resisting it with senseless brutality, then in my opinion it will not be difficult for it to re-organise its industrial structure in three or four years and restore its economy to the level it had prior to the war in Bangla Desh. The raw material base of most of its industries is either domestically produced agricultural goods or materials imported from abroad. Over the last 20 years it has also developed quite a substantial intermediate goods industry, and whatever might be said of the method by which it built up this industry, the stocks, the knowhow and the factories are there. Quite a number of the factories, it is true, are very inefficient by international standards. If inputs and outputs were valued at international prices, a number of them would be found to be running at a loss. A more rational policy would be to close these uneconomic units and streamline such industries, and once the investment has been made and the necessary interim dislocation accepted, recovery would not be impossible. Except for cotton textiles, I do not think it would be very difficult for West Pakistan to absorb these surpluses within its own economy in a couple of years' time. For the time being there would be a glut but since in a developing economy effective demand is seldom a major strain on the output of industrial products, it should not take very long to come out of the temporary excess. Furthermore, in most of these industries the rates of profit are very substantial and the excess supplies may be eliminated rather quickly if the business community willingly accepted some cut back from these very high profits.

The main difficulty in West Pakistan is going to be the shortage of resources because of the sharp fall in foreign exchange earnings, the overwhelming part of which had been used in the past to bolster the economy of West Pakistan. Even now a very large proportion of essential commodities are imported and their absence could bring the economy quickly to a standstill. East Pakistan has been contributing 45 per cent to 50 per cent of the total foreign exchange earned by Pakistan in recent years, and the loss of that would have to be matched by a corresponding inflow of foreign resources, which can only come on terms other than commercial until the economy gets going again. In the present state of the world, assistance on the scale required is not unobtainable but it can only come if the countries approached for it are more willing to accept than they have been lately that West Pakistan is not seeking foreign aid, whether economic or military, simply in order to impose a grim colonialism upon East Bengal.

SHADOW OF THE BIG POWERS

V. P. DUTT

THE DRAMATIC developments in East Bengal are in fact neither so surprising nor so unexpected as they seem on the surface. They are the logical outcome of the manner in which India was divided under the British policy of divide and rule and as a result of the failure of the Indian National Congress leadership to prevent the Muslim masses from being influenced by the politics of communalism. Pakistan provided the odd example of a country with two wings, separated from each other by a thousand miles of the territory of another country, being kept together by the bond of religion, rather tenuously as it has now been proved.

The British withdrew from India after the country had been partitioned and the two states of India and Pakistan had been created. But they continued to lay down the policy line in regard to the sub-continent for the Western countries for a long time to come, especially for the United States. The most important ingredient of the British policy was that there ought to be some kind of parity, or at the very least balance, between India and Pakistan. This was the view which the British transmitted to the United States; Washington

acted on it for many years to come and to some extent does
so even now. The maintenance of a balance of power between
India and Pakistan has been the guiding principle of both
the United States and Britain in their policies towards this
part of the world.

At the same time the United States became rapidly involved
in the cold war and communism became for it the great
menace to be fought all over the world, the great determinant
of U.S. foreign policy, the prism through which the U.S.A.
saw the world. United States policy towards the Indo-Pak
sub-continent came to rest on four pillars: balance of power
between India and Pakistan; assistance to both India and
Pakistan with a view to preventing their possible collapse as
functioning and viable countries; propping of Pakistan as an
anti-communist base against the Soviet Union and China on
the one hand and to meet possible anti-Western subversion
in West Asia on the other hand; using Pakistan as a sensitive
lever of pressure against India. The United States gradually
came to be preoccupied with the problems of communism
and did not wish to see India go under a communist revolution.
In fact in the initial period the United States entertained the
hope that India might play the role of a leader of the anti-
communist countries of Asia.

The *New York Times* commented editorially on October
13, 1949, that Washington wants India to be a bulwark
against communism and a great and growing market..." [1] The
then Secretary of State, Dean Acheson, said in an address to
the United States Congress that India was at a critical point
in its history. The recent elections had shown some very
startling things. Although the Congress Party won by a substantial majority, the Communist Party showed "unexpected
strength", especially in certain localities. He revealed that
the advice of U.S. observers was that unless the newly
independent government under Prime Minister Nehru could
show substantial progress in economic development over the
next five years, the likelihood was that in the next elections
"the democratic forces would be endangered either by extremists of the right or by the communists. But disaster does

1. The *New York Times*, Editorial, 13 October, 1949.

not need to happen in India. With our help they can succeed,"[2] he said.

However, as India showed less and less desire to play such a role in Asia and as the area of difference between New Delhi and Washington expanded over the question of China, the peace area in South-East Asia and non-alignment, the United States turned more and more towards Pakistan as a reliable ally against communism and national liberation struggles. Pakistan encouraged the United States to believe that it was a faithful friend, although everyone except the United States knew that Pakistan's only concern was enmity with India. In the anti-communist wave in U.S.A. Washington chose to turn a blind eye towards this and sought to make Pakistan an important anti-communist base in Asia. The United States Secretary of State, Dulles, spoke of his impressions about Pakistan before the House Committee on Agriculture and said, "One of my clearest impressions was that of the outstanding and sincere friendship which the leaders of Pakistan feel for the United States. I was greatly impressed with their understanding of world problems. You know they will resist the menace of communism as their strength permits. You know that Pakistan and the United States have commonly supported the same views in the United Nations and Pakistan was a tower of strength on the Japanese treaty." [3]

The friendship with Pakistan, while fitting into the anti-communist framework of the foreign policy of the United States, could also be used to influence and exercise pressure against India, and this aspect did not go unnoticed in Washington. Thus the attitude of the United States towards Kashmir gravitated towards indirect support of Pakistan. As Gordon Graham of the *Christian Science Monitor* noted, "Pakistan, at present the loser in Kashmir, has everything to gain and nothing to lose by close cooperation with the West Britain especially welcomes a reliable Muslim ally, and concerned over its waning influence in Egypt and Iran, appears anxious to build up a strong economic and military liaison

2. Speech at the 82nd Congress, 2nd Session. *Mutual Security Act of 1952; Hearings before the Committee on Foreign Relations*, United States, page 14 to 15.

3. United States House, 83rd Congress, Ist Session, Committee on Agriculture, Hearings, *Wheat (Aid) to Pakistan* (Washington, 1953), p. 6.

with its increasingly powerful Muslim Commonwealth member. Whatever the reason, Pakistan's case in Kashmir is more favoured in the United States and Britain today than India's. That Pakistan, faced with Indian de-facto control of Kashmir has said to the West, 'You need a strong Pakistan; to be strong Pakistan needs Kashmir' cannot be dismissed as an expansion of this apparent propaganda victory." [4]

The same logic led the United States to get more and more involved in the support of Pakistan, culminating in large-scale military assistance. One aspect of this policy was highlighted by Harold Stassen, at the time Director of the Mutual Security Administration, who defended military aid to Pakistan in these words: "We feel that Pakistan may well become a second Turkey. They are a stalwart people and will provide an anchor in the Near East. We have one anchor in the Eastern Mediterranean, pretty well developed, and at the other end of the Near East, the protection has been very weak. Now we are beginning to develop what may be an opposite anchor in Pakistan. It may be a slow process, things might be upset there, but that is the direction in which we are moving." [5]

President Eisenhower, announcing the decision to give military aid to Pakistan on February 24, 1954, tried to allay the apprehensions expressed in India and other countries by assuring them that aid would be given specifically on the condition that the equipment, materials and services provided would be used solely to maintain the recipient country's internal security and for its legitimate self-defence, or to permit it to participate in the defence of the area of which it is a part. The recipient country would also undertake that it would not engage in any act of aggression against any other nation. He held out the assurance that if the aid was misused and resulted in aggression by the recipient country, the United States would take appropriate action against such aggression.

These assurances notwithstanding, it was obvious that Washington had moved all the way to full support of Pakistan, underwriting its economy and maintaining a generous flow of military hardware, which was subsequently estimated at a

4. *Christian Science Monitor* (Boston), August 2, 1951.

5. U. S. House, 83rd Congress, 2nd Session, Sub-Committee of the Committee on Appropriations, Hearings, *Mutual Security Appropriations for 1955* (Washington, 1954), p. 17.

billion dollars in value. Its implications for India are well-known and need not be repeated here but what was not earlier realised may now be clarified: that for the United States, Pakistan really meant West Pakistan. East Pakistan, inhabited by the majority of Pakistan's population, never entered U.S. calculations. Perhaps in a way that was a reality even within Pakistan, for West Pakistan came to regard itself as co-terminous with the state of Pakistan, and the people of East Bengal came to be treated as second class citizens. But East Pakistan was never enthusiastic either about the anti-communist role assumed by West Pakistan on behalf of Pakistan or about its consuming enmity against India.

It was in East Pakistan that opposition to military aid developed later among the various left-inclined groups and particularly among the intellectuals, teachers and students. A united front against the ruling Muslim League Party was organised under the leadership of Maulana Bhashani and in the elections in 1954 it overwhelmingly defeated the League, proof enough of East Pakistan's opposition to alliance with the United States and military assistance from the country.[6]

The opposition Front demanded the resignation of the Central Government, dissolution of the Constituent Assembly, acceptance of Bengali as a national language on a par with Urdu, autonomy for East Bengal, abolition of visas for travel between India and East Bengal and the repudiation of American military aid. These developments led to a crisis at the Centre itself climaxing in the establishment of autocratic rule in West Pakistan. These developments focussed the attention of the United States on the tensions existing in Pakistan. Many eyebrows were raised in the United States and fresh questions were asked about the strength and reliability of the ally. But Washington did not as yet undertake any reappraisal of its basic policies.

For many years the United States looked up to Britain for a lead on the problems of the Indo-Pak sub-continent as that country was supposed to be more knowledgeable about them in view of its past intimate experience as a colonial power. The United States and Britain often concerted their forces and acted in close consultation in regard to South Asian

6. *New York Times*, 31 March, 1954.

issues. On the question of Kashmir, the United States and Britain often came forward with joint resolutions, which were generally acceptable to Pakistan but unacceptable to India. Even at the time of the Chinese aggression against India in October, 1962, the American President and the British Prime Minister met at Naussau to hammer out a joint approach and to take common steps in this crisis.

President Kennedy's initial response was one of immediate and open hearted support to India. In a confidential communication, President Kennedy urged Ayub Khan of Pakistan to make a friendly gesture to India in her hour of grave peril and suggested that Ayub Khan might privately inform India that Indian troops posted in Kashmir could be safely withdrawn to fight against Chinese invaders. Such an offer, Kennedy suggested, would win Indian goodwill and probably put them in a favourable frame of mind for a settlement of the Kashmir issue.[7] Of course, the appeal was brushed aside by Ayub Khan.

While Washington was initially inclined not to impose any conditions on the assistance proposed for India in the wake of the Chinese aggression, the British thought otherwise and seem to have impressed upon the Americans that the time was ripe for compelling India to make concessions to Pakistan on Kashmir. Thus before the American and British representatives, Harriman and Sandys, came to India to pursue the question of assistance, the British point of view had prevailed and Nehru was obliged to send the Indian Foreign Minister, Swaran Singh, to Pakistan for talks on Kashmir with the Foreign Minister of Pakistan, Bhutto.

There was some change in the United States policy towards the Indo-Pak sub-continent during the short-lived Kennedy regime. President Kennedy showed greater awareness of the position of India and attached greater importance to her role. There was some thaw in the cold war and the United States began moving away from extreme positions and reactions, particularly in regard to nonalignment. It was no longer regarded as immoral to be nonaligned as in Dulles time. China's conflict with India helped to bring India and United States somewhat nearer. At the same time Pakistan improved its relations not only with the Soviet Union but also with China.

7. Theodore Sorensen, *Kennedy*, (London, 1965), page 664.

The crunch came in September, 1965, during the Indo-Pak war. Pakistan freely used all the arms given by the United States against India despite earlier assurances to the contrary. As one U.S. writer put it: "Yet Washington had not even taken a strong and immediate verbal stand against Pakistan's extensive use of sophisticated military equipment in this war though such an outright violation of the aid agreement left America's 1954 guarantee to India in shambles. This violation of earlier agreements, however, did make future acquisitions of new American equipment more doubtful and led Pakistan to turn—with some success—to Peking for tanks and jet combat planes." [8]

It is interesting to note U.S. reactions to the growing friendship between Pakistan and China. Although some apprehension and misgivings were expressed, the United States showed considerable patience and restraint in its relations with Pakistan. Even some understanding was expressed about the need for Pakistan to improve relations with Peking. As AID Chief Bell told the Senate Committee on Foreign Relations in April, 1965: "Now, the judgement that has been made continuously, and is still our judgment, is that despite the flirtation between the Pakistan and Communist Chinese, it remains true that the Pakistan Government is a strong Government and a strong anti-Communist Government and that it is valuable to the United States to have some minimum or some significant military forces in Pakistan with which we are in continuous association, which could be used under certan circumstances." [9]

Although President Kennedy had said at one time, "Pakistan never understood that America's alliance with them was aimed at the Communists and not at the Indians",[10] Washington now took the view that Pakistan's move for friendship with Peking was born out of enmity against India and that it did not fundamentally represent an anti-U.S. move. Therefore the United States need not be frightened by it.

Many assumptions of U.S. policy were knocked out one by one. Pakistan proved to be neither as stable nor as strong as

8. Fred Greene, *U. S. Policy and Security of Asia* (New York) 1968, 138.
9. U. S. Senate 89, First Session, Committee on Foreign Relations, *Foreign Assistance Act of 1965* (Washington, DC, 1965).
10. Theodore Sorensen, *Op.cit*, p. 664.

the United States had fondly hoped. The hope that Pakistan would be the bastion of anti-communism in this part of the world was given a deadly blow by Pakistan's overtures to the Soviet Union and growing friendship with Peking. The assurance that the arms gifted to Pakistan would not be allowed to be used against a third country was demolished in 1965. But the attempt to maintain an artificial balance between India and Pakistan has not been abandoned, and this explains the difficulty that Washington is having in adjusting itself to the changing situation in South Asia. But of this later.

The Soviet Union started from the other end. Pakistan's participation in the military alliance system of the Western powers, which was chiefly directed against Moscow, and India's opposition to military alliances had created a condition in which Moscow found itself nearer to India than Pakistan. India's opposition to the cold war, her efforts in the cause of peace, her unequivocal support to the struggles for freedom in Asia and Africa and her advocacy of the peace area contrasted with Pakistan's avowed anti-communist stance, support .to the United States on most issues and her lukewarm attitude towards the struggles for independence. Even though Pakistan's attitude was based on the requirements of an alliance which she hoped to use against India, as a consequence of the differing nature of Pakistan's and India's policies, the Soviet Union's relations with India gradually developed while those with Pakistan remained cool. Soviet support to India on Kashmir proved crucial.

A qualitative change in India's relations with the Soviets came when Khrushchev and Bulganin visited India in 1954. They began giving aid to India which rapidly grew, and announced Soviet support to India on Kashmir, which was subsequently underlined by the Soviet representative in the Security Council when he said: "The Soviet Union's view and its basic premise is that the Kashmir question has in actual fact been settled in association by the people of Kashmir itself, and they considered their territory an integral part of the Republic of India." [11]

Economic relations between India and the Soviet Union

11. *Official Records of the Security Council of the United Nations,* supplement for Jan-Feb. March 1957, Dec. S/3779, mtg 770, pp. 38-9.

grew apace. The Soviet Union became India's second biggest trade partner after the United States, and its share in India's foreign trade increased from 2.2 per cent in 1956 to approximately 13 per cent in 1969. Trade between the two countries is now expected to grow approximately by six per cent a year. Its escalating conflict with China inevitably brought the Soviet Union still closer to India. A new dimension was added to Indo-Soviet relations when the Soviet Union began to give India increasing quantities of military hardware on rupee payments.

Until 1964, Moscow's relations with Pakistan did not show any substantial improvement. In fact the Soviet leader, Mikhail Suslov, chided the Chinese leaders for joining hands with Pakistan in an anti-Indian alliance. In a report to the Central Committee of the Soviet Communist Party, Suslov said: "While allowing relations with India, which as everybody knows is not a member of military blocks, to deteriorate sharply, the Chinese leadership has factually made an alliance with Pakistan, a member of SEATO and CENTO, which are threatening the peace and security of the Asian peoples. It is a fact that, having discarded their 'revolutionary phrase-mongering' the Chinese leaders are steering a course that can hardly be regarded as compatible with the principled position of the socialist countries with respect to imperialistic blocs.

"The approach of the Chinese leaders to the choice of friends and allies is strange, to say the least. How is it possible, it may be asked, to abuse and slander the socialist countries and the communist parties and at the same time, with the whole world watching, shower compliments on the reactionary regime in Pakistan? That is simply beyond one's understanding.

"Can any one believe that the rapprochement with Pakistan was prompted by the interests of the development of the revolutionary anti-imperialist struggle of the people of Asia, about which the Chinese leaders talk so much?" [12]

But within a year of Suslov's stinging denunciation of Peking, the process of normalization of relations between the Soviet Union and Pakistan began. Pakistan was assiduous in her efforts to live down the U-2 incident and to assure Moscow that her

12. Suslov's Report on "Sstruggle of the CPSU for the Unity of World Communist Party", *New Times*, No. 15, Supplement, 1964, p. 50.

membership of an American military alliance was in no way a reflection of hostility to the Soviet Union but was directed purely against India so far as Islamabad was concerned. Moscow too began to respond to Pakistan's overtures, gave economic assistance and followed it up with military aid. By 1969, the Soviet Union—although still way behind the munificence shown by Washington—had become the second biggest source of economic assistance to Pakistan. Till the time of the visit of Kosygin to Pakistan in April, 1968, the Soviet Union had provided $ 176 million to Rawalpindi for various purposes, including $ 30 million for oil exploration and $ 11 million for the import of Russian agricultural machinery. Kosygin underwrote a steel plant with a capacity of a million tons at an estimated cost of $ 300 million, an atomic power station and further assistance in oil exploration and other enterprises.

The Indo-Pakistan war and its aftermath saw the full development of this Soviet policy. The Soviet Union was extremely unhappy about the conflict, which it felt would only weaken the already weak economies of the two countries and promote instability in Asia.[13] Premier Kosygin appealed for an end to the fighting and withdrawal of forces behind the 1949 cease-fire line and offered Soviet good offices for a settlement. He demarcated the Soviet position from other outside forces on the plea that they (Western and Chinese had nothing in common with the interests of the Indian and Pakistani peoples, whereas the Soviet Union was seeking to promote normalization of relations between India and Pakistan. The Soviets particularly denounced Peking's attempts to fan the flames of war and its "ultimatum" to India. Finally, after the acceptance by the two sides of the U.N. resolution on cease-fire, the Soviets succeeded in bringing them together at Tashkent and through benevolent neutrality and gentle pressure secured what subsequently came to be known as the Tashkent Agreement.

The Kremlin was impelled by many important factors to take this extraordinary interest in the affairs of the sub-continent and to make efforts in a difficult and delicate situation to mediate between India and Pakistan and to bring them together in simultaneous friendship with Moscow.

Geography was, no doubt, one factor. The Soviet Union is

13. Observer in *Pravda*, 24 August, 1965.

in more immediate proximity to the Indo-Pak sub-continent than to south-east Asia where China acts as a physical barrier to Soviet activity. With the intensification of the conflict with China and the realisation that China was more a rival than an ally, Moscow was confronted with the problem of seeking fresh options and new friends. Moscow turned towards India in an early response to this problem. India's position as the second largest country in Asia made it a natural first choice, and other factors helped. There are no national irritants between India and the Soviet Union, like the border problem between the Soviet Union and China; the Soviet Union has not given any open support to countries with which India is in conflict; on the other hand there is a steady convergence of the national interests of the two countries. Therefore friendship and cooperative relations developed quickly between them.

Soviet efforts in Pakistan can also be seen as part of the same search for options and friends. Soviet overtures and a larger Soviet presence reduced Pakistan's dependence on Washington, eroded the usefulness and mischief-making capacity of the American military alliances and, at the same time, dissuaded Pakistan from getting too close to Peking. These were regarded as useful gains for the Soviet Union. But Moscow's ultimate hope and greater expectation was that the triangular alliance between Moscow, Islamabad and New Delhi would provide a powerful counter-balance to the ambitions of China and the actions of Washington, and if Moscow played its cards well in Vietnam, neither China nor America would be able to knock together an opposing alliance as effective as this one.

The Soviet Prime Minister, Kosygin, said in Moscow in May, 1965, on the occasion of the visit of the late Prime Minister Lal Bahadur Shastri that, "when the Soviet Union tries to improve its relations with other countries, it does not do so at the expense of Soviet-Indian friendship. We know that the Government of India adheres to the same line." [14] On the other side of the coin a *Pravda* commentary said: "Strengthening the ties between the USSR and Pakistan must be regarded as a part of the general policy of ensuring peace in Asia and throughout the world. We should like Soviet-Pakistan relations, like our traditional friendship with India, to be a stabilizing factor in the

14. *Pravda*, 16 May 1965.

situation in Asia and to contribute to the normalization of relations between Pakistan and India." [15]

Inevitably the Soviet effort at friendship with Pakistan was matched by an equally zealous effort at maintaining friendship with India. The Soviets were careful in not giving the impression that their need for friendship with Pakistan would work to the disadvantage of India. They used their growing influence in Pakistan on the side of peace, moderation and the easing of tensions. They were not free with advice to India for making concessions on Kashmir—as many other countries were.

Moscow stepped up its economic assistance to both India and Pakistan. It adopted a posture of studied but benevolent neutrality and all its efforts were aimed at preventing an eruption of the hot flames of war. But Moscow's eventual hope about this triangular equation was predicated on the assumption that Islamabad would be willing to play the game and join in creating this new balance in south-east Asia. There was no evidence that Pakistan had any intention of doing so. Moscow was counting without the fact that for Pakistan any balance must be a balance against India and that it had no interest in a balance against either China or the United States.

For India there was some cause for anxiety in this situation. The Soviet Union had not befriended Pakistan at the expense of friendship with India. But situations could radically and dramatically change. At one time Moscow had given total support to India and had given up its option with Pakistan but now had managed to reactivate it. Given the premises, some amount of Soviet arms assistance to Pakistan had also become inevitable.

The Soviet decision to supply arms to Pakistan produced consternation in India and gave the country a sudden jolt. India took the only possible view of it, that this aid would only be used against India. But it was in some ways a logical development of the new Soviet strategy. This was the real meaning of Tashkent, and Moscow's decision was inherent in the logic of the approach it had adopted since then. If the Soviets wanted to draw Pakistan closer to them, they had to open another source of arms for it. The new Soviet strategy was

15. *Ibid.*, 24 August, 1965.

directly related to the split with the Chinese and the compulsions of Asian politics.

The break with Peking had suddenly left the Russians high and dry on the Asian continent. The Americans had their bases of operation, acquired through various allies. The Chinese, with their huge land mass, effectively functioned as a major independent power in Asia. But Moscow hoped to work its way through New Delhi and Islamabad for a major Asian role. If the Soviets could keep this potentially important sub-continent with them—neither attached to Peking nor too close to Washington but dependent mainly on Soviet assistance Moscow would have established a highly viable counterpoise to Peking's and Washington's alliances. For this it was necessary to cultivate friendship with both India and Pakistan. It followed that the Soviets would give military aid to Pakistan and thus draw it away from the other two adversaries, particularly from Peking.

The Soviet policy had been reshaped after careful deliberation. Moscow was not making a choice between India and Pakistan; in fact, the conviction in the Kremlin was that there was no need for such a choice. Moscow hoped to weather the storm in India and then succeed in its objective of keeping both India and Pakistan with it. The strategy was to give as much assistance to Pakistan as was necessary to bring it closest to Moscow, and to provide even more massive aid to India so as to retain the special Soviet presence in India. Moscow had shrewdly calculated that this kind of assistance would not be available to India from anywhere else and would, therefore, serve to cushion the shock of arms supplied to Pakistan.

The difference between Soviet and U.S. approaches was that the Soviet Union had not tried to create an artificial balance between India and Pakistan. The Soviet concern was not Pakistan versus India, but it was hoped in Moscow that it would carry both Pakistan and India along with it. For the Soviet Union the major force in south Asia was still India, but it now believed that it could best function in Asia with the simultaneous friendship of Islamabad and New Delhi.

Pakistan's apparent success in diplomacy could be ascribed to its ability to convince Peking, Washington and Moscow that since its only enemy was India, its friendship with one big power was not directed against another. In Peking it pleaded that it had to turn to Washington and then to Moscow in order to acquire strength against India, and if Peking wanted to reduce Pakistan's dependence on the other two, it should come forward and help. It argued in Moscow that it was forced to lean on Washington at one time and then on Peking because of its security needs in relation to India and that the Soviets could help mitigate this dependence by giving aid to Pakistan. Similar explanations were offered in Washington in defence of closer relations with Peking and Moscow. All three of them, Moscow, Peking, and Washington, played the power game in Islamabad, each trying to expand its own presence and to contain that of the other two. But the calculations of the three powers and their assumptions were not the same. I have already explained the development of U.S. and U.S.S.R. policies towards the Indo-Pak sub-continent. We can now take a look at the development of the corresponding Chinese policy.

There can be no doubt that the Indo-Pakistani equation was a factor in Chinese policy, in Asia in general and in this part of the world in particular. In the initial period, soon after the induction of the new Communist Government, the Chinese Communists, like the rulers of the Soviet Union and Communists all over the world suspected both India and Pakistan of being imperialist stooges". and being freshly revolutionary they were not well disposed towards these "reactionary bourgeois" governments. But very soon, in fact surprisingly soon, the Chinese discovered the need for friends and realized that their national interests demanded a more flexible approach. The American encirclement had to be countered, the new regime had to consolidate its power, the isolation had to be ended. This could only be done by enlarging their circle of friends and by utilizing the "contradictions" between the West and the newly emerging Asian countries. Significantly, the Chinese first chose India as the country to be befriended.

To some extent, the Chinese were responding to the Indian eagerness to build friendly ties with China to ensure peace with a neighbour and to promote peace in Asia. But the Chinese also recognised the fact that they needed the friendship of the second largest nation in Asia which was refusing to be pressurized into a military alliance and which was pursuing an independent foreign policy. This friendship could mitigate the isolation and encirclement of China and advance China's cause in the world. Inevitably, the Chinese were suspicious of Pakistan for its membership of SEATO and the Baghdad Pact (now the CENTO) and were quite critical of Pakistan's foreign policy stance. To Pakistan the threat was from India alone. Pakistan took the risk of offending China by joining a military alliance which was ostensibly directed against China, but it made every effort to explain to the Chinese that Pakistan had no enmity towards them and its sole reason for joining the alliance was to acquire military muscle against India. It is common knowledge that during the Bandung Conference Mohammed Ali of Bogra, then Prime Minister of Pakistan, reassured the Prime Minister of China, Chou En-lai, that Pakistan had no quarrel with China and that its confrontation was only with India.

Despite its hostility towards a West-oriented Pakistan, it is obvious that China was well aware of the possibilities inherent in the Indo-Pakistani conflict. Whereas India took the slogan of abiding friendship between China and India a little too literally and seriously, China showed particular awareness of the likelihood of a future conflict with India and the need to leave room for manoeuvre in the Indo-Pakistani equation. And so, despite violent and vehement denunciation of SEATO and criticism of its non-Western members for toeing the imperialist line, China left the door open in its approach to Pakistan for future manoeuvres. This was especially evident in the Chinese stand on Kashmir; it practiced ambivalence in order to keep some elbow room in case of a future showdown with India. Privately, China assured India that it fully understood and appreciated India's position with regard to Kashmir, but publicly it contented itself with blaming the imperialists for the trouble and appealing to India and Pakistan to settle the dispute peacefully. [16] When a senior official of the Government of India raised

16. See, for instance, the joint statement issued on February 5, 1957, by Chou En-lai, Prime Minister of China and S.W.R.D. Bandaranaike, Prime Minister of Ceylon, expressing their distress at "the unfortunate situation that has arisen in the dispute between Pakistan and India in regard to Kashmir" and appealing to the two countries "in their own as well as in the wider interests of Asian-African solidarity to strive further for a peaceful settlement of the problem". The *Hindu* (Madras), 6 February. 1957.

the issue with the Chinese Prime Minister, Chou En-lai replied that China believed that the people of Kashmir had already expressed their wishes in regard to their future status. [17] However, when Sino-Indian relations soured, China began to make unfriendly statements on the Kashmir issue. When India protested against them, China turned round and asked whether India could point out any Chinese leader or official spokesman who had accepted the Indian position on Kashmir. [18] Clearly, China had grasped early the opportunities offered by the hostility between India and Pakistan and for utilising them later and hence was prevaricating over Kashmir.

But, as stated earlier, during the period 1952-58, China was suspicious of Pakistan's intentions and alliances, and at least upto 1957 was more concerned with retaining India's friendship. In fact, the induction of President Mohammed Ayub Khan through a military coup d'etat brought about a sharp deterioration in the relations between China and Pakistan. He was regarded as being more pro-American and anti-Chinese than all former rulers of Pakistan, and his military agreements were acknowledged as a threat to the security of India also. When Pakistan signed a bilateral military agreement with the United States on March 5, 1959, which spoke of U.S. and Pakistani "determination to maintain their collective security and to resist aggression, direct or indirect",[19] Peking was quick to condemn it as an act of blackmail not only against China but against India, too. The agreement did not specifically refer to "communist aggression", as all previous defence agreements of this kind did, but made a general reference to "aggression, direct or indirect".

The Pakistani authorities triumphantly claimed that the wording was deliberate and that it covered "aggression" from such quarters as India. At the time, Peking put upon it the same construction as India did—that it was a double-edged sword, one side aiming at China, and the other at India. *Jenmin-Jih-pao*, the mouthpiece of the Communist Party of China,

17. Government of India, Ministry of External Affairs, *Notes, Memoranda and Letters Exchanged between the Governments of India and China*, White Paper 6 (New Delhi, 1962), pp. 96-97.

18. Chinese note of May 31, 1962. *Ibid.*, pp. 99-102.

19. See the Department of State Bulletin (Washington, D.C.) Vol. 40, pp. 416-18.

commented sharply in an editorial that, "the United States and its followers have also put forward a new idea that resistence to any direct or indirect aggression includes noncommunist aggression. This clearly shows", it added, "that these new pacts are directed not only against the socialist countries but are, in the first place, also a threat to such nationally independent neighbouring countries like India, Iraq, and Afghanistan. These new military pacts will enable the United States to intensify its suppression of the national liberation movements and threaten peace and security in Asia." [20]

The military agreement, Peking said in another comment, enabled the United States to build large-scale military bases openly in Pakistan and to use them against neighbouring, peaceloving countries. It noted that newspapers in Pakistan did not "even attempt to cover up the hostile provisions of the bilateral agreement aimed against India and Afghanistan."

Obviously Peking regarded Pakistan's military alliance as constituting a clear and present threat to India. Peking also turned sharply on Ayub Khan not only for his friendship with the Americans but also for his attempts to drive a wedge between India and China. *Jen-min-Jih-pao* chided the "Pakistani Foreign Minister and other responsible officials" for making repeated statements at home and abroad "slandering the Chinese people, interfering in China's internal affairs, sowing discord in the relations between China and India and agitating for the cold war".[21]

The attack on Ayub Khan was sharp and minced no words. "Since the Ayub government came to power last year," Peking said, "the Pakistan government has been following a policy of increased dependence on the U.S. In March this year, Pakistan signed a bilateral military agreement with the U.S. under which the United States is allowed to use armed forces and establish bases in Pakistan, thus taking a step further in turning Pakistan into a U.S. military springboard in South-east Asia. This agreement seriously threatens the security of the Soviet Union, China, India, Afghanistan, and other Asian countries and strengthens U.S. control over Pakistan. This policy of the Pakistani ruling clique is diametrically opposed to the interests

20. *Jen-min Jih-pao* (Peking), editorial, 7 March, 1959.
21. *Jen-min Jih-pao*, 23 July, 1959.

of peace in Asia and is also opposed to the national interests of Pakistan".[22]

But as the border conflict between India and China widened, Peking changed its tune about Pakistan. Pakistan had all along been trying to assure Peking that it had no enmity against China and that its only enemy was India. Though the Chinese leaders were somewhat dubious about Pakistani professions in the early period, the growing confrontation with India made them receptive to Pakistan's overtures. References to Pakistan became warmer in their propaganda, and those to India more and more hostile. Delegations started going to and fro and communications between the two countries became more intimate.

The process of growing collusion between China and Pakistan was pushed further by President Ayub Khan's visit to Peking when the red carpet was rolled out for him. Instead of complaining about the role of Ayub Khan, as Peking had done till as late as 1959, the Chinese now declared that ever since Ayub Khan came to power, relations between China and Pakistan had been improving and Ayub was given a great deal of credit for it. In the biographical notice published prominently by Peking newspapers, Ayub Khan's role as a loyal servant of the British army was underplayed and his contribution to the development of Pakistan's "national independence" and friendship with Peking was lauded.

Pakistan's massive armed attack in the Chhamb area across the international frontier on September 1, 1965, aiming at detaching Kashmir from the rest of India, forced India to launch a counter-offensive in defence of its territorial integrity. Peking maintained a studied silence during the first few days, but as the war started going against Pakistan, the veil of silence was lifted and Peking came out in fullthroated support of Pakistan and threatened India with dire consequences if it continued its "aggression" against Pakistan.[23] Peking took no notice of Pakistan's membership of SEATO and CENTO and the colossal acquisition of arms, heavy and light, from the United States. Pakistan was now portrayed as an innocent, small, progressive country being subjected to the pressures and bullying of "reactionary" India, "imperialist" America, and "revisionist"

22. *Ibid.*
23. See the Chinese Government statement of September 7, *Peking Review*, No. 37, 10 September, 1965.

Russia. It almost looked as if Pakistan was not fighting with American but with Chinese weapons.

Chinese leaders said that Pakistan's cause was just, that it was the victim of aggression, that India had invaded Pakistan at the behest of America (and perhaps of Russia too), and indicated their determination to give moral and material support to Pakistan. [24] They also reaffirmed their backing for Pakistan on the Kashmir issue and denounced the Soviet Union for its "shameful" support of India in its "expansionist" designs. The evidence also points to a considerable, even though secret, coordination of effort between China and Pakistan in so far as their moves against India were concerned.

As Indian forces prepared for a further push towards Lahore and Sialkot, Chinese troops increased their aggressive activity on the northern frontier and as usual, charged India with provocatively intruding into Chinese territory, particularly in the Sikkim area, building bunkers there and stealing Chinese yak and sheep. Finally, China gave India a 48-hour ultimatum (subsequently extended by another 48 hours) to remove bunkers from the Chinese side of the border allegedly constructed by India and to return Chinese yak and sheep, or else face grave consequences. It is significant that this threat came when UN Secretary-General, U Thant, had come to India after talking to Pakistani leaders in Rawalpindi and that President Ayub Khan delayed his reply to the Secretary-General's suggestion for an immediate cease-fire and made his negative response coincide with the Chinese ultimatum.

This crude threat from China was clearly designed to compel India to let up pressure on Pakistan, to assure Pakistan that China was a reliable friend, and to disrupt U Thant's mission of bringing about a cease-fire. It is equally significant that at the end of the expiry of the second ultimatum, the Chinese announcement that India had demolished the military structures on the Tibetan side of the border with Sikkim (thus providing an excuse to Peking for backing out of its threat) came just before Z. A. Bhutto, Pakistan's Foreign Minister, announced to the Security Council, Pakistan's acceptance of the cease-fire. Obviously each had foreknowledge of the other's moves.

24. *Observer*, "Indian Reactionaries' Expansionism", *Ibid*. Also see Foreign Minister Ch'en Yi's statement. *Ibid*. No. 41, October, 1965.

This Sino-Pakistani collusion continued after the Indo-Pakistani war and, if any thing, became closer, with Peking giving substantial arms aid to Pakistan and keeping an aggressive posture on India's northern frontiers. Both China and Pakistan hoped that by maintaining a "second front" against India, sufficient pressure could be mounted against her to compel her to yield ground in the unresolved issues between them and India; they also hoped that India's prestige in the international community, particularly in the Asian-African world, would thus be further undermined. Pakistan hoped that India might thus be put on the run in regard to Kashmir, and China that India would be obliged to supplicate for peace with it, totally destroying her influence in Asian-African affairs. Of course, each of these two states was playing its own game and there was no complete identity of interests. China would expect Pakistan to fit into its overall strategy and, therefore, would not match its limitless verbal support to Pakistan with actions to help its SEATO ally. But India as the common enemy provided a useful meeting ground.

Like the other two big powers, Peking also based its policy towards Pakistan on the assumption that the Central Government, representing essentially the West Pakistani military-bureaucratic elite, was the only force to deal with and that this elite spoke for the whole of Pakistan. Although there was a sizeable pro-Peking group in East Pakistan, led by Maulana Bhashani and subsequently Toaha, Peking routed its policy mainly through Islamabad and did not give any overt recognition to the movement in, and problems of, East Bengal. In fact, this group was utilized by the Pakistani government for obtaining support from Peking and the former President, Ayub Khan, sent Maulana Bhashani to Peking to persuade the Chinese Government to be more forthcoming in its support to Pakistan against India. Peking was not lacking in its response but it concentrated on relations with Islamabad and gave no public indication of awareness of the separate identity of East Bengal.

None of the big powers realised the gravity of the problem in East Bengal because none of them paid much attention to that area. All of them found it prudent to base their policies on relations with the military-bureaucratic elite in Islamabad. They all seem to have been taken unawares by the magnitude of the crisis in Pakistan, and were unprepared to respond to it promptly and in any determined manner. This attitude can only be understood if related to the context of their basic policies towards the Indo-Pak sub-continent. The real reason why they are finding it so painful to react to the developments in Bangla Desh is that their basic approach to the sub-continent did not provide for this contingency.

The reaction or the lack of it by the big powers has run true to their preception of their objectives and interests in this region. The United States and Britain had not only put all their eggs in the basket of the military rulers of Pakistan but their policies were predicated on the preservation of a balance between Pakistan and India. If East Pakistan became independent, there would be nothing left of the so-called balance. West Pakistan alone could not be expected to provide that parity with India which they were seeking to confer upon Pakistan. The emergence of Bangla Desh posed fresh problems and challenges for the the United States. What kind of internal and foreign policies would this new state adopt? Bangla Desh would certainly be at the very least a non-aligned country, friendly to India and willing to carry on commerce and trade with both sides of the struggle in the international arena, and certainly with India. The uncertainty that it implied for U.S. policy is obvious.

At the same time the United States could not just turn a blind eye to the unprecedented violence and bloodshed in which the military rulers of West Pakistan were indulging in East Bengal. As Krishna Bhatia, the *Hindustan Times'* correspondent in Washington put it: "If the U.S. Administration is maintaining a steady posture of diplomatic sangfroid and propriety in respect of East Pakistan's freedom movement, its moral dilemma is showing like the proverbial spinster's slip." [25] The dilemma was that on the one hand the authorities had not raised their voice against the barbaric manner in which the people of East Pakistan were being crushed by the Yahya regime and on the other hand the situation placed an increasingly difficult burden on the U.S. conscience because U.S. arms, given to Pakistan for defence against communism, were being used to put down the popular movement led by elected representatives of the majority of the people.

25. *Hindustan Times,* 6 April, 1971.

The State Department declared subsequently that the U.S. Administration was "reviewing" its 1967 arms and foreign policy which enabled Pakistan to buy spare parts and non-lethal military equipment from Washington. But a State Department spokesman, Charles Bray, at the same time indicated that pending a decision on the question, Pakistan's purchases under this agreement were being allowed to be delivered. [26] In 1967 the United States Government had allowed Pakistan to buy spare parts and so-called non-lethal military equipment. This had enabled Pakistan substantially to recover from the damage it suffered in the 1965 conflict with India.

Reports from the United States said that privately the Administration was letting it be known that it was putting some pressure on Pakistan to bring about a peaceful solution of the problem with the followers of Sheikh Mujibur Rehman. The United States Government was in fact coming under increasing domestic pressure to take some measures to stop the genocide in Pakistan and at the very least not to allow its arms and equipment to be used by Pakistan to suppress its own people brutally. Influential newspapers published harrowing accounts of the bloody repression in East Bengal. A number of influential U.S. Senators, including Senators Kennedy, Fulbright and the Republican Senator Saxbe, among others deplored the killing in East Bengal and appealed to the United States Government to prevent the use of American arms to break down the people of East Bengal. The Senate Foreign Relations Committee passed a resolution urging the cessation of all aid to Pakistan until a peaceful solution was found to the problem of East Bengal and the rulers of West Pakistan ended their military action there. Influential segments of unofficial opinion in the United States as well as in England are exercised over the use of massive military power and American arms against the people of Bangla Desh. They are also aware of the futility of West Pakistan's policy of murder in East Bengal. The *New York Times* has called it the year of the vulture in East Bengal. Both the *Times,* London, and the *Manchester Guardian* have acknowledged that the bridge between the two halves of Pakistan is now unbridgeable and that, despite repression and temporary military successes, West Pakistan will not be in a posi-

26. *Hindustan Times,* 14 April, 1971.

tion permanently to occupy East Bengal. The Labour Party has taken a strong stand against the atrocities and suppression in East Bengal.

The developments in Bangla Desh pose many awkward problems for the Soviet Union too, which had also banked heavily on the military administration in West Pakistan. The Soviet policy of evolving a triangular combination of Moscow, Islamabad and New Delhi for meeting the problems of Asia would be in danger of a collapse if East Bengal broke away from Pakistan. The Soviets could also have been suspicious of the pro-Peking group in East Bengal and unsure whether the leadership of the movement in East Bengal would pass into its hands.

All this could explain the initial hesitation of the Soviet Union. It was a major policy problem and posed painful choices. But as the popular nature of the revolt in East Bengal became more evident and as the truth about the genocide in East Bengal filtered through, the Soviet Union's stance towards Islamabad became stiffer. Soviet newspapers began carrying accounts of the killings in East Bengal and the revolt of the people. On April 2, the Soviet press called for a political settlement and expressed concern at the army action. *Komsomolskaya Pravda* said: "These army actions are nothing other than crude arbitrariness and violence which arouses the sincere concern of the Soviet people." [27]

The most authoritative statement of the Soviet assessment came in the well-known message by the Soviet President, Nikolai Podgorny, to President Yahya Khan "insistently appealing for the adoption of the most urgent measures to stop the bloodshed, the repression against the population of East Pakistan, and for turning to methods of a peaceful political settlement." The Soviet President said rather sharply that "Soviet people cannot but be concerned by the numerous casualities, by the suffering and privations that such a development of events brings to the people of Pakistan. Concern is also caused in the Soviet Union by the arrest and persecution of Mr. Mujibur Rehman and other politicians who had received such convincing support by the overwhelming majority of the population of East Pakistan at the recent General Elections." Lest there should be accusations of interference in the affairs of Pakistan, the Soviet

27. Reuter dispatch in the *Hindustan Times*, 3 April, 1971.

President emphasized that Moscow was guided by "the generally recognized humanitarian principles recorded in the Universal Declaration of Human Rights and by concern for the welfare of the friendly people of Pakistan."[28] The Soviet Union clearly implied that the military administration of Islamabad had violated the humanitarian principles recorded in the Universal Declaration.

Quite clearly the Soviet Union had made a new assessment of the balance of forces in Pakistan. They had come to the conclusion that the struggle in East Bengal enjoyed the fullest measure of support by the people of East Bengal. The Soviet sympathy for the people of Bangla Desh was therefore made unmistakably clear. The Soviet Union's future action would be determined by developments in East Bengal but its sharp reaction left no room for doubt that it regarded the struggle in East Bengal a people's struggle.

One other vital element entered the decision-making processes of the Soviet Union, which enabled it to take this stand. In its policy towards the Indo-Pakistan sub-continent, the Soviet Union had not been motivated, unlike China and the United States, by the need for Pakistan providing an artificial balance against India. The Soviets wanted to carry both Pakistan and India together with them, but when it came to the crunch they regarded India as the principle factor in south Asia as well as in their general Asian policy. Friendship with India was therefore primary, and it was this underlying approach of the Soviet leaders that made it possible for them to risk the whittling down of their influence in Islamabad and to take a position which was fairly sympathetic to the struggle in Bangla Desh.

Peking's dilemma was especially painful and embarrassing. Ideology pointed in one direction while national interest, as Peking's leaders saw it, in another. The Chinese leaders had been proclaiming to the world that the most important determinant of their foreign policy was support to peoples' struggle. They had in fact claimed that it was this which distinguished their foreign policy from the foreign policies of the Soviet Union and many other countries of the world. By any yardstick the struggle in East Bengal fulfilled the qualifications of

28. *News and Views from the Soviet Union,* Information Department of the USSR Embassy in India, New Delhi, 6 April, 1971.

125

being a national and people's struggle. But the power game that Peking was playing in the Indo-Pak sub-continent obliged the Chinese Government to forget ideology in favour of the power game.

That the dilemma was highly embarrassing may be responsible for the fact that Peking's comments have been unusually limited and scanty, and whatever comments have been made have generally taken the line of denouncing India for "inter ference" in the internal affairs of Pakistan.[29] In fact the developments in Bangla Desh and Peking's reaction to them have shown that Peking's policy towards South Asia is still determined by its attitude towards India. The most important element in this policy since 1959 has been the need to find in Pakistan a counter-weight against India. The events in Bangla Desh could knock the bottom out of this policy because shorn of East Bengal which constitutes the majority of the population of Pakistan and contributes the greater part of its resources, West Pakistan could hardly be considered a counter-weight against India. Peking was not prepared to undertake any fundamental and agonizing reappraisal of its policy in this subcontinent, and therefore political considerations triumphed over ideological demands.

The most authoritative and informative reaction of Peking can be found in the letter of Chou En-lai of April 12 to General Yahya Khan. There are two elements in this message which need to be taken note of and which provide a clue to Chinese policy. Firstly Chou-En-lai said: "In our opinion the unification of Pakistan and the unity of the people of East and West Pakistan are the basic guarantees for Pakistan to attain prosperity and strength." Clearly the "unity" of Pakistan was to be maintained even in the face of a popular struggle against autocracy and repression by the military administration of West Pakistan. The rule of the military administration over the whole of Pakistan was preferable to the emergence of Bangla Desh which might be non-aligned and socialistic but which would obviously be friendly to India.

Secondly, Chou En-lai accused India of interference in the affairs of Pakistan. He said "We have noted that of late the Indian Government has been carrying out gross interference

29. *Jen-min Jih-pao*, 11 April, 1971.

ın the internal affairs of Pakistan by exploiting the internal problems of your country. And the Soviet Union and the United States are doing the same, one after the other. The Chinese press is carrying reports to expose such unreasonable interference, and has published Your Excellency's letter of reply to Podgorny."[30]

Peking's intention obviously was to continue its campaign against India and the Soviet Union. The Chinese accusations have been refuted by East Bengal leaders and intellectuals. Even those who were prominently pro-Peking have shown dissatisfaction over Peking's attitude. No less a person than Maulana Bhashani, leader of the pro-Peking National Awami Party, refuted the charge of Indian interference. In a telegram to the Chinese leaders, Maulana Bhashani reminded them: "The ideology of socialism was to fight oppression, and if the Chinese Government did not protest against the atrocities of the military junta, the world may think that you are not the friend of the oppressed people."[31]

The awkwardness of Peking's dilemma is further demonstrated by the curious fact that whereas Pakistan gave immense publicity to the message of Chou En-lai, Peking did not release it for internal consumption. Peking has come out in support of General Yahya Khan and as long as it does not review its fundamental policy of supporting Pakistan as a counter-weight against India, it will be difficult for it to adopt any other policy. However, Peking has paid a heavy price for adopting this attitude towards the struggle in Bangla Desh. It has lost face among the people in East Bengal as well as annoyed the pro-Peking intellectuals in India, and few in the world would believe now that Peking's policy is determined by ideological considerations. Whether this will promote a reappraisal in Peking remains to be seen.

One can visualize a hypothetical situation in which the struggle in Bangla Desh turns more and more "extremist" and turns towards China for support and succour. In that case China could change its policy and encourage divisive forces in both parts of Bengal. This is an apprehension expressed by many in India and abroad. However, in the recent crisis China has done little to endear itself to the people of Bangla Desh. Any

30. Text of the Message in *Pakistan Times*, 23 April, 1971.
31. *Hindustan Times*, 23 April, 1971.

change in Peking's attitude can only flow from an abandonment of some of the basic elements in its approach towards south Asia. One cannot envisage an easy and prompt turn in Peking's policy.

To sum up and conclude, the emergence of Bangla Desh, the butchery and repression in East Bengal, and the heavy inflow of refugees into India have upset the calculations and considerations which went into the making of the policies of the big powers towards this sub-continent and towards Pakistan. But their response is conditioned and determined by their larger approach towards this region. China has been motivated since 1959 by hostility towards India and therefore remains indifferent to the national struggle in East Bengal. As the purpose of the Soviet Union has been to win the friendship of both India and Pakistan and maintain close relations with India, Moscow has been able to show greater flexibility and to express sympathy for the people of Bangla Desh. The United States' primary motivation is not hostility towards India and Washington does not wish to see Indian democracy scuttled, but it has relied heavily on the ruling group in West Pakistan, and along-with Britain, its effort has been to maintain a balance between Pakistan and India. Therefore, it would rather continue to deal with the military bureaucratic elite in West Pakistan. Nixon is under considerable pressure from the military establishment and a section of the State Department bureaucracy to bail out Pakistan from the economic disaster facing it regardless of what happens in East Bengal. Similar logic has governed British policy. But there is a rising pressure of public opinion both in the United States and Britain against the atrocities inflicted on East Bengal. As a result the two governments may attempt a compromise of kinds, a hesitating policy and an attempt to continue to stake some presence in Islamabad through a measure of aid and assistance. It is only the final success of the struggle in Bangla Desh which can bring about a transformation in Western policy. But international opinion can be mobilised to deny Western arms to Pakistan and severely to limit any other kind of aid from being given to West Pakistan until it ceases its warfare against the people of East Bengal.

As for India a question which could have been a matter between the people of East Bengal—constituting the majority of the population of Pakistan—and the small ruling group in

West Pakistan has become an issue between India and Pakistan because of the heavy influx of refugees into India. Already over two and a half million have crossed over from East Bengal into India and at this rate nearly eight to ten million people may do so. In the world's history there is no parallel to this unprecedented flight of the people into another country to protect themselves from the tyranny of their government. The influx would put an intolerable burden on Indian economy and cannot be accepted by India as a permanent, accomplished fact. India would have to take every measure available to it to compel Pakistan to accept the responsibility of enabling the refugees to go back to their permanent homes. If the struggle of the people of Bangla Desh succeeds, as it must sooner or later, then the refugees would be automatically enabled to return and live in peace and honour in their own country. But in the meantime, if the struggle remains a protracted one, Pakistan cannot be allowed to ruin India's economy by driving out its own people.

TREMORS IN WEST PAKISTAN

DEWAN BERINDRANATH

TEN WEEKS after the reign of terror let loose by it, the West
Pakistan army remain completely dependent upon the iron
heel for keeping down the movement for Bangla Desh. That
is because of its triple failure so far to crush the support
which the Awami League still enjoys among the people, its
failure to organise even a puppet civilian regime which could
claim at least some legitimacy, and its failure to mobilise the
political strength of West Pakistan behind what has been so
far a naked military onslaught upon the civilian population
of Bangla Desh. It has succeeded in disrupting political life
in Bangla Desh. But it has not been able to put any substitute in its place; even the establishment of a civilian administration eludes it so far. On the other hand dangerous fissures
have appeared in the links between political life in the two
wings as well as in the polity of West Pakistan.

Elimination of the leadership in East Bengal was one of the
major objectives of the offensive by the West Pakistani army.
Preparations for it were made well in advance; lists of the
Awami League activists were ready by the middle of March.
But a large number of the "wanted" men were able to escape

because of "leakages" in the intelligence services. That is why West Pakistan papers have complained that "treacherous elements had entered into the police force who have always been misleading the authorities," [1] the reference was to Bengalis who manned the intelligence services at lower levels. This perhaps accounts for the escape of a large number of important leaders like Tajjudin Ahmed, Sayeed Nazrul Islam and Mushtaq Khundkar.

The army was able to disrupt the Awami League machine because the resistance groups lacked advance coordination and could not build it up in the face of the sudden army offensive, for which the Awami League leaders were completely unprepared. Student leaders and their followers thus became helpless victims of the overwhelming barbarity by the army in Dacca University and in campuses in Rajshahi and Chittagong. But as soon as they were able to recover their breath, Awami League leaders were not only able to meet, but also to work out a plan of action and form a provisional government which has become the rallying point and an emotional link between the struggle in the past and in the future.

It is not yet clear why the provisional government headed by the acting President Sayeed Nazrul Islam is composed only of Awami League elements. Other parties which are opposing the regime like the two factions of the National Awami Party and Bengal National League of Ataur Rehman, did not find a place in it. This might be due to a certain lack of understanding among various resistance groups, but the reason could also be expediency. At any rate the pronouncements of Maulana Bhashani and Muzzaffar Ahmed, who head the pro-Peking and pro-Moscow factions of the National Awami Party, respectively, confirm that all the nationalist and leftist elements are united in opposing the Yahya regime.[2] That is why the army, which had not touched National Awami Party activists in the first round, later started a systematic drive to liquidate them as well. Most of the National Awami Party leaders succeeded in going underground, which accounts for the resistance put up to the army in areas like Chittagong and Mymensingh, where the National Awami Party was particularly strong.

1. *Nawa-e-Waqt*, Lahore, 28 April, 1971.
2. *Hindustan Standard*, Calcutta, 16 April, 1971.

The more extremist and younger elements were thrown into confusion by the Chinese support to the Yahya regime; they were hoping till recently that Peking would help the revolutionaries rather than a discredited military dictatorship. Newspaper reports also suggest that Mohammad Toaha the extremist leader, who had broken away from Maulana Bhashani's N.A.P. and was at one time talking of "armed revolution" on Naxalite lines, went into political retirement later.[3] But by the middle of May it became clear that the influence of the extremists elements was on the decline and fears that the leadership of the movement would slip out of the hands of the Awami League to the Naxalites were not fully justified. If substantial help reaches the provisional government headed by Sayeed Nazrul Islam from friendly countries, its hands will be strengthened not only in its fight against the Yahya regime, but also against any attempt at disruption by the extremist elements.

Support for the Awami leadership from groups like that of Bhashani, Muzzaffer Ahmed and Ataur Rehman indicates the emergence of a broad-based united front of all the leftist and democratic elements. The extremist elements can make a dent in this only if India adopts an apathetic attitude.

One result of the military action has been the complete severance of inter-wing links between the leadership of parties which have a base in both wings. The two factions of the National Awami Party, the Council and the Convention Muslim Leagues, and groups like the Jamat-e-Islami and the Pakistan Democratic party, though small, had an inter-wing character which has now been lost. Unwittingly, thus, the Yahya Khan regime has completed the ideological and organisational separation of political organisations in the two wings by suppressing legitimate political activity.

Maulana Bhashani's National Awami Party had actually lost its links with the West even before the military action. In January this year Maulana Bhashani declared that he would fight for an independent and united Bengal through the struggle of peasants and workers and would have nothing

---

3. Indian newspaper reports, flashed with apparent approval by Pakistani newspapers, *Jung*, Karachi, *Nawa-e-Waqt*, Lahore, and *Imroze*, Lahore, 29 April, 1971.

to do with West Pakistan.[4] The West Pakistan National Awami Party, which enjoyed some support in trade unions and in certain rural pockets of West Punjab, met at Lahore after the announcement by Bhashani and decided to form a group of its own. Well-known trade union leaders such as Mian Ibrahim, Mrs. Kaneez Fatima, C. R. Aslam and Arif Iftikhar, son of the late Mian Iftikhar-ud-Din, declared that they would keep the National Awami Party in the West wing intact independently of Maulana Bhashani.[5]

The pro-Moscow faction of the National Awami party went through a different process of severance from the East. Following military action in Bangla Desh, the President of the East Pakistan National Awami Party, Muzzaffar Ahmed, declared his full support to the provisional government. The National Awami Party President, Wali Khan, who is also the leader of the majority in the North West Frontier Province, felt embarrassed by this forthright declaration, disowned Muzzaffar Ahmed and reiterated his stand that his party was in favour of maximum provincial autonomy but was opposed to secession.[6] Following this demands were made in the West Pakistan press that Muzzaffar Ahmed and his associates should be formally expelled from the National Awami Party but Wali Khan resisted the demands on the plea that conditions in East Pakistan were such that no authentic version of the pronouncements of Muzzaffar Ahmed and others could be obtained and it would not be proper to take action against them without giving them a chance to state their case. Whatever the merits of this controversy, it underlines again the tremendous distance which has been created between the politicians of West Pakistan and East Bengal by the army's action and the resulting difficulties in the way of any future attempt to normalise political relations between the two wings.

Compared to the leftist parties, right wing groups have fared better. The Jamat-e-Islami, the Council Muslim League, the Convention Muslim League and the Pakistan Democratic Party, after appearing to approve Sheikh Mujib's call for a united struggle, hastily retraced their steps and the first declaration in support of the military regime came from Nurul Amin,

4. *Jung*, Karachi, 16 January, 1971.
5. *Nawa-e-Waqt*, Lahore, 2 February 1971.
6. *Pakistan Times*, Lahore, 16 April, 1971.

leader of the Pakistan Democratic Party and the only non-Awami leader to be elected to the National Assembly from East Bengal. Nurul Amin, it may be recalled, was the first Muslim League Chief Minister of East Bengal, but was trounced by an Awami League student leader in the provincial assembly elections in 1954. There is some evidence however to suggest that things did not go well between Nurul Amin and the military regime. This was perhaps due to the fact that Nurul Amin could not go the whole hog with the genocide perpetrated by Yahya Khan. It soon became clear that the military government was not too happy with Nurul Amin and was trying to find other elements as civilian props to its policy of repression. The so-called peace committee which was set up by the military rulers to counter the nationalist movement was not headed by Nurul Amin but by Maulana Farid Ahmed, who had lost his security deposit to an Awami League candidate. Other politicians whom the regime wanted to make use of were Hamidul Haq Chowdhary, a former Foreign Minister of Pakistan, A. K. Saboor, leader of the House in the National Assembly during the Ayub regime, and Fazlul Qadar Chowdhary, a former speaker of the National Assembly, all of them nonentities in the political field.

As the army started entrenching itself in urban areas, it became more and more evident that it could not maintain a purely colonial rule as an occupation army. It felt the need for a civilian link between the army and the people and it thought of setting up a civilian provincial government.[7] A number of so-called peace committees were set up in Dacca and various other towns, with which a number of non-Awami League elements, especially from the right wing groups, were associated. But inspite of a good deal of propaganda, they remain helpless appendages to the military regime; their value in terms of the association of the people with the occupation forces is less than nominal.

Going by the experience of the peace committees, one can say that a civilian government, even if one is sought to be foisted upon the people by the military regime, will have little credibility among the people, because of the cruelties of the military dictatorship. By making the Awami League the main

7. Front-page report in *Jung*, Karachi, 17 April, 1971.

target of its wrath, the army has destroyed the chance of a compromise with other dissident elements also. The chances of a civilian government being set up in West Pakistan are also bleak. The party position is not clear in any province except Punjab. Even in Sind, the position is complicated by the fact that Bhutto's Peoples' Party enjoys only a two-vote majority, which could be disturbed at any time. Bhutto's own equation with General Yahya Khan is shrouded in so much mutual suspicion that the military regime is most unlikely to hand over power to him only to facilitate some sort of a face-saving device in East Bengal. In N.W.F.P. and Baluchistan, it would in any case be most difficult to find "proper persons" to whom power may be handed over.

To get over such difficulties, the military regime could decide to bring in civilian ministers as advisers to the Governors. But politically strong elements in West Pakistan have been strenuously opposed to the military picking up some politicians without reference to the elected representatives of the people. Popular opposition to such nominations was one of the reasons why General Yahya Khan was practically forced to disband his civilian cabinet immediately after the elections. Therefore the conclusion appears to be inescapable that even if the military regime is able to overpower resistance in a large area of Bangla Desh, it will have no option but to retain its colonial character for a long time to come. The complete destruction of the Bengali middle-classes has robbed the regime of the possibility of making a compromise with elements who might have had a vested interest in peace and stability in the area.

In the wake of the fighting in Bangla Desh, various solutions have been proposed by pro-establishment elements in West Pakistan. The most notable is the one put forward by Z. A. Sulehri, Editor of *Pakistan Times,* who has proposed division of East Bengal into three provinces[8] to rob East Bengal of the appeal of a unified nationalism and to create vested interests in the three provinces which could be played off against one another. The size of the three proposed provinces would be comparable with that of Punjab and Sind; this would provide further leverage to the Central government to deal with the challenge of a unified Bangla Desh.

8. *Pakistan Times,* Lahore, 5 April, 1971.

Another suggestion has been made by orthodox elements that the joint electorate accepted for East Bengal should be scrapped and new elections held on the basis of separate electorates. Abdul Qayum Khan of the Convention Muslim has said that the joint electorate was mainly responsible for the Awami League victory and is in any case an anomaly in an Islamic State.[9] The Jamat-e-Islami has also advocated fresh elections on the basis of separate electorates on the plea that non-Muslims should not participate in political activity in an Islamic state; they could only ask for protection of life and property. They have not cared to ponder over the fact that the margins by which most of the Awami League candidates won were so high that the minority vote of the Hindus would not make much difference in a future election. In any case it is extremely doubtful whether the military regime can risk holding elections even on the basis of separate electorates in an area where the revolt of at least 95 per cent of the population has become an acknowledged fact.

The same can be said about the idea of dividing Bengal into three separate provinces. It envisages long drawn political activity with some semblance of normalisation. Vested political interests can take root in the separated states only when there is some revival of political activity. But allowing political activity in any part of East Bengal is like belling the cat for the Pakistani rulers.

One of the major problems for the regime in West Pakistan is the partial success of its own propaganda regarding East Bengal. Since it has been repeatedly asserting that there is hardly any resistance left in East Bengal, any measure to solve the problem in a drastic manner is not likely to get much popular support. Rawalpindi is thus faced with a dilemma. Neither can the people be told that the situation is extremely bad, necessitating complete suspension of political activity and the re-imposition of Martial Law in the two wings of the country. Nor can the revival of political activity be allowed because that would eventually mean power passing from the hands of the military rulers.

The effectiveness of military control in Bangla Desh depends to a very large extent on developments in West Pakistan the

9. *Morning News*, Karachi, 10 April, 1971.

home base of the army's power. A few basic points therefore need to be emphasised about West Pakistan. Firstly, it would be wrong to talk about the West Pakistani reaction as if the whole area were a unified entity. Emotionally, it would be more realistic to talk about Punjabi, Sindi, and Baluchi or Pathan reactions. Secondly, some areas of West Pakistan, having been the main beneficiaries of the exploitation of East Bengal, cannot be expected to show much sympathy for the struggle for Bangla Desh. Thirdly, because of various political, economic and geographical factors, some powerful elements in West Pakistan, especially the Punjabis and a section of Pathans, have come to develop a vested interest in the unity of Pakistan. This vested interest has been buttressed through relentless ideological propaganda. Islam, with all its extra-national ramifications, has been used as part of this propaganda. It did not have much of an impact in East Bengal but it has become an important factor in the thinking of a large section of West Pakistani intelligentsia.

The military junta has been playing upon the fear in Punjabi and Pathan minds that the separation of East Bengal would start the process of the disintegration of West Pakistan, which would in turn be swallowed by Hindu-India.[10] India is a far more potent factor for Punjabis and a section of the Sindis and Pathans than it ever was for the East Bengali. The Kashmir problem has always remained a symbol of confrontation with India for the man of urban West Punjab. The war of 1965 reinforced this sense of confrontation, especially in Punjab while weakening it further in East Bengal. Military leaders, most of whom belong to extreme West Punjab and the eastern parts of North-West Frontier Province would naturally like an atmosphere of tension to be kept up to justify the large defence budget and the economy of East Bengal to be permanently available for supporting it. The association of a large number of Punjabis, Baluchis and Pathans with the army gives them added loyalty to a united Pakistan.

Keeping these three factors in mind, one could have expected a very strong outburst of sympathy and support in West Pakistan, especially in Punjab and N.W.F.P. for the Yahya regime in its confrontation with East Bengal. But nothing of the

10. *Nawa-e-Waqt*, Lahore 13 April, 1971.

sort happened in fact. As a first reaction, a sullen silence descended upon West Pakistan. This underlined one of the most glaring failures of the Yahya regime in handling the present conflict. Inspite of all its efforts, the ruling junta was not able to turn this fight into a confrontation between East and West Pakistan. It remained what it actually is, a fight between a military dictatorship and 75 million people.

At the same time, a large number of people, described merely as "dangerous and anti-social elements", have been rounded up in Karachi, Lahore and Lyallpur. Those arrested include trade union and student leaders. Some of them are known to be followers of Tariq Ali, who belongs to a leading West Punjab family and has issued a statement from London hailing the fight for freedom in Bangla Desh. Under his leadership a powerful section of West Pakistani residents in Britain have also lent their full support to Bangla Desh.

At a meeting held recently in London a number of West Pakistani students, teachers and trade union workers are reported to have decided to form a "West Pakistan Association for Solidarity with Bangla Desh". The Association aims at educating public opinion in West Pakistan about the real nature of the conflict in Bangla Desh and mobilising resources for the help of the freedom fighters.

A leaflet issued by the Association says "The military rulers of West Pakistan have been exploiting West Pakistani masses as much as they have been exploiting the people of Bangla Desh. They have imposed severe censorship on all forms of news and have turned the whole country into a vast concentration camp. It is the sacred duty of every conscious West Pakistani to fight against such a dictatorship, which represents only a handful of feudalist and monopoly interests in Pakistan and is pursuing policies totally inimical to the interest of the people". Prominent West Pakistanis connected with this pro-Bangla Desh movement include, besides Tariq Ali, Air Commodore Janjua, a former General Manager of Pakistan International Airways, the well-known writer and intellectual, Hamza Alvi and a trade union leader, Naseem Bajwa.[11]

Indications of dissatisfaction with the policies of the military

11. Press Asia International, report from London, Broadcast by All India Radio 9 May, 1971.

138

rulers in East Bengal have also come to light in West Pakistan itself. Yusuf Khattak, former opposition leader in the National Assembly and General Secretary of the Convention Muslim League, has disclosed in a statement that "even now there are very powerful elements in West Pakistan, whose sympathies are totally with Sheikh Mujibur Rehman and other anti-state elements in East Pakistan."[12] The government he adds, must take action against those who have been actively engaged in sabotage in West Pakistan and have been trying to incite trouble among the students, workers and peasants.

Abdul Qayum, President of the Convention Muslim League, has also warned the government against "the danger of pro-Mujeeb elements gaining ground in the North West Frontier Province, Sind and 'Azad Kashmir'." Such statements followed the discovery of sizeable left-wing activity in the western region.

The Communist Party of Pakistan, which has continued to be illegal since 1952, appears to have become active and is openly trying to canvass support against the regime. A declaration by the "Sind Provincial Committee of West Pakistan" has been widely circulated all over West Pakistan in the form of a handbill. The declaration, which has also been circulated among West Pakistanis living in the United Kingdom has been printed secretly. It strongly criticises the military rulers. It says: "The cowardly junta of army generals has launched a campaign of mass slaughter against the Bengali people with the aid of arms bought with money earned by the people's hard labour. The defeat of the army junta is inevitable. Bullets, jails, conspiracies, repression and barbarism have not been able to stop the march of the people earlier, and they will not succeed now either".[13]

Another significant statement has been circulated by the Baluchistan Students' Organisation (BSO). It calls on the people to get ready for the final assault on dictatorship. It pointedly recalls the various campaigns of terror and repression that Pakistani rulers have launched against the people of Baluchistan and Pakhtoonistan ever since Pakistan came into existence. These included aerial bombings against the Baluchi people and repeated firings upon the Pakhtoons. "The only crime of

12. *Jung*, Karachi, 13 April, 1971.

13. Handbill issued in London and printed in *Motherland*, New Delhi, 4 May, 1971.

the people of Baluchistan and Pakhtoonistan was to ask for provincial autonomy", says the BSO. The statement says the people of East Bengal have taken a leading part in this struggle and have made "unparalleled sacrifices for the cause of democracy and autonomy."

There have also been reports of industrial unrest in West Pakistan. Trouble has been reported from Lyallpur, Lahore and Karachi. Just as the army went into action in East Bengal, clashes between workers and the military occurred in these cities. In Lyallpur and some parts of Karachi, curfew had to be imposed and the army issued "shoot at sight" orders. The workers have been agitating not only for fulfilment of certain industrial demands, but also for restoration of the right to strike and repeal of Martial Law measures which have deprived them of all means of peaceful protest.[14]

Important leaders of Bhutto's Peoples' Party have been involved in a movement of agrarian unrest. Mukhtiar Rana, a member of the Pakistan National Assembly, and a leading figure in the Punjab branch of the Peoples' Party, has been arrested and charged with sedition. Two members of the Provincial Assembly belonging to the Peoples' Party have also been charged with incitement to violence and lawless activities. The Punjab branch of the People's Party threatened to launch a mass movement of landless tenants by way of forcible occupation of the land of big landlords if suitable land legislation was not enacted within a month. These are indications of unrest in West Punjab over the prolongation of military rule and continued exclusion of popular representatives from the government.[15]

Reports of clashes between landlords and tenants in the North-West Frontier Province which were initially suppressed by newspapers under official bidding, leaked out when the Governor and Martial Law Administrator of NWFP, Lt. General K. M. Azar Khan, had to admit them in an address to tribal leaders and prominent citizens in Peshawar in the middle of April. Addressing them, the Governor was reported to have expressed his "deep anguish over the regrettable dis-

14. *Jung*, Karachi, 26 April, 1971.
15. See for example the statement of Mr. Mustufa Khar, General Secretary of the Punjab Branch of Peoples' Party, *Pakistan Times*, Lahore, 16 April, 1971.

turbances in the Tangi Charsadda area". This was a centre of strong activity by Khan Abul Ghaffar Khan's Red Shirt movement; now his son, Wali Khan, is active here.

The Governor also disclosed that following the armed clashes between tenants on the one hand and landlords and the police on the other, large scale arrests were made to "restore law and order". He promised 'reasonable compensation' to a large number of victims of the clashes who have apparently lost their lives. *Pakistan Times* further quoted the Governor as having told the gathering that the Government had decided to post a punitive police force in the areas. The residents of the area, he said, would have to bear all the expenses of the force, including their salaries. He also thought "this would minimise the incidence of disturbances". He regretted the fact that tenants had refused to pay taxes to the government and due share to the landlords.

He gave a stern warning to the tenants that such non-co-operation and lawlessness would not be allowed. Commenting on the Governor's statement, Abdul Quyum, President of the Pakistan Muslim League, said in Peshawar that large scale agrarian unrest on the pattern of the "land grab movement" in India had been planned in N.W.F.P. and Baluchistan by what he called "pro-Mujib elements".

It would be far-fetched to suggest any direct link between the war in Bangla Desh and agrarian and industrial unrest in West Pakistan. But it would be naive to ignore the significance of such developments occuring at a time when the rulers are trying to convince the people that the nation is locked in a life-and-death struggle against Indian infiltrators and Hindu-imperialists. Such expressions of dissent in West Pakistan present a complete contrast to the scene during the war in 1965, when the Ayub regime was able to achieve a tremendous sense of national unity. The war in Bangla Desh on the other hand has given further momentum to the demand for regional autonomy and secular nationalism which is being made in the West Pakistan provinces.

Early in May, G. M. Sayed, the well-known Sindhi leader, was arrested and detained along with the leading Sindhi poet, Sheikh Ayyas, and a number of leading workers of his Sind United Front on charges of "fomenting anti-national sentiments among a section of the people". G. M. Sayed, former Chief Minister of Sind and also an important member of the Working Committee of the All-India Muslim League under Mohammed Ali Jinnah, had organised the Sind United Front a few months ago. At the beginning of this year he went on a pilgrimage and when the war started in Bangla Desh pro-establishment newspapers reported that he had gone abroad to organise help for Sheikh Mujibur Rehman and to foment trouble in Sind.[16] Bhutto, for reasons of his own, lent his support to the efforts of the regime to blacken G. M. Sayed's image by demanding at a public meeting that "all elements sympathetic to the Awami League ideas and opposed to the ideology of Pakistan should be crushed". G. M. Sayed has been a strong supporter of Sheikh Mujibur Rehman though the main grudge which the regime had against him was the popularity of his ideas of secular nationalism among the Sindhi youth; he was accused of coining the 'Jai Sind' slogan which gripped the imagination of Sindhi students almost in the manner of 'Jai Bangla' in Bangla Desh.

How powerful the movement he initiated has become is illustrated by the large scale language riots in Hyderabad (Sind), Mirpur Khas and other areas in October last year and January this year. The main cause of the riots, which claimed over fifty lives according to official estimates, was the demand that Sindhi should be made the medium of instruction as well as of official work in Sind. Pakistani newspapers have been complaining against the 'Jai Sind' movement whose main objective is to attain complete autonomy for Sind and to ensure proper development of Sindhi language and culture.[17]

Demands have also been made that a proper place be given to other regional languages in West Pakistan, as against Urdu, which is supposed to be the mother tongue of only about five per cent of the total population. Punjab, which had hitherto been considered the bastion of the conservative ideas has witnessed a great deal of cultural upsurge as a result of the Punjabi movement. Some of the leading Urdu poets belonging to Punjab have lent their support to the demand that Urdu be replaced by Punjabi as the medium of administration and education.[18]

16. *Jung*, Karachi, 4 April, 1971.   17. *Jung*, Karachi, 10 April, 1971.
18. A notable Urdu writer, who has lent his support to the Punjabi Movement is Faiz Ahmed Faiz the foremost Urdu poet and a Lenin Prize winner.

Political frustration has grown with the realisation that the war in East Bengal must mean continuation of military dictatorship in West Pakistan too. The regime is obviously not in a position to oblige those who have been suggesting that pending a settlement in East Bengal, power should be transferred to popular representatives in West Pakistan. Bhutto, who was instrumental in creating many an alibi for the military regime, appears to have been ditched once again. He had been demanding restoration of civil liberties and the initiation of a process of democratisation. He has asked for transfer of power before June 30.[19]

The demand has been rejected by the men who rule and are determined to continue to rule. While Bhutto has been ignored, a large number of his followers have been put behind the bars. They include the General Secretary of Punjab People's Party, two members of the National Assembly and three of the Provincial Assemblies. While no one would today consider Bhutto's bona-fides as a democrat with any degree of seriousness, his campaign for democracy does indicate the existence of widespread discontent among the people over the continuation of military rule. This lends ominous potentialities to the present fractious posture of the People's Party chief, who till yesterday was acting like a public relations officer of the military regime.

Simultaneously with the assumption of such an anti-establishment posture by Bhutto, reports have come of simmering trouble in the palace. Many knowledgeable foreign correspondents have hinted about the possibilities of a shake-up in the military junta. The existence of a hard core of hawks with intimate relations with Bhutto has been commonly talked about. No one can deny the possibility that just as this hard core egged General Yahya Khan to precipitate matters in East Bengal, it may force him to take a desperate step towards India as well to attract world attention and to play the final gamble for consolidating public support at home.[20]

It is not only a coincidence that the report of the so-called Commission of Inquiry into the hijacking of an IAC plane

19. *Pakistan Times*, Lahore, 4 May, 1971.
20. Of special interest are reports by the *London Times* and *Washington Post*, and the Associated Press of America, filed by their correspondents from Karachi in the last week of April.

came just at the moment when reports of a challenge to the regime were becoming more and more frequent. The commission accused the two hijackers of being Indian agents. This fantastic allegation that the hijacking was managed and manipulated by India has an important aspect; it shows a desire on the part of the military rulers to place Bhutto in the wrong. The Commission's "disclosures" about the alleged Indian hand in the hijacking came at a time when Bhutto was again clamouring for power. He has been closely associated with the "Kashmir Liberation Front", headed by Maqbool Butt who had claimed credit for the hijacking. Maqbool Butt had boasted a day before the hijacked plane was destroyed that the "whole of Pakistan is in our palm". The destruction of the plane was hailed as the victory of the pro-Bhutto elements in West Pakistan, particularly in the Pakistan-held Kashmir. Significantly, the commission has accused Maqbool Butt also of being an Indian agent and he has been arrested. The so-called inquiry report has thus been used as part of the power game which is going on in Rawalpindi.

Along with the desire for democracy and for regional autonomy, economic factors are also contributing to the isolation of the military establishment from the people in West Pakistan. The price of the war in economic terms has already started telling upon the daily life of the people. Newspaper reports suggest a sudden spurt in prices, especially of items like tea, tobacco, jute goods, fish, mutton and betel leaf. The prices of tea and tobacco are reported to have risen by about a hundred per cent, and the betel leaf has become a rare item of great luxury. 'Newsweek' has estimated that military operations in East Bengal cost Islamabad about two million dollars a day (Rs. 1.50 crores).[21]

By the middle of May the rise in prices had started attracting even official attention. General Yahya Khan convened a conference of Military Governors to discuss the food situation.[22] While in Washington, M. M. Ahmed, economic adviser to the Pakistan President, disclosed that his country did not have food stocks for more than three or four months.[23] Even the semi-

21. *Newsweek*, New York, 17 May, 1971.
22. *Pakistan Times*, Lahore, 22 April, 1971.
23. *Times of India*, New Delhi, 12 May, 1971.

144

officially owned *Pakistan Times* had to admit that prices of essential commodities had arisen by about fifty per cent following the war in Bangla Desh, creating "the worst crisis in Pakistan's history".[24]

Devaluation of the Pakistan rupee by 100 per cent appears to be imminent in view of pressure by the World Bank and the International Monetary Fund. Further promises of aid to Pakistan are reported to have been withheld pending this step. *Newsweek* quoted the market price of the Pakistani rupee as Rs. 11.20 per dollar about the beginning of May, while its official value continued to be Rs. 4.76 per dollar.[25] The reason for this spectacular fall in the value of the currency is not merely the complete stoppage of exports from East Bengal; it is also due to an increasing demand for import of commodities which were hitherto supplied by East Bengal. The price of newsprint for example is reported to have risen three-fold following the fighting in Bangla Desh. Wreckless inflationary steps by the military regime to help it pay for the war have also added to the dismal picture on the economic front.

The whole spectrum of political and economic life in West Pakistan is thus beset with pressure which may force the regime to resort to anti-Indianism. But seeing the mood in West Pakistan, it can be said that even this may not work. Indo-phobia yielded remarkable results in the 1965 war but has failed to click this time. Except for a handful of leaders no one has come out in support of the stand of the military regime on any of the important internal or foreign issues because the continuation of military rule in East Bengal cuts at the very root of the aspirations of the West Pakistanis. They had overwhelmingly voted in favour of a democratic political order and had categorically rejected all those who had any association with the military regime. Bhutto's victory in Punjab and Sind can only be explained in terms of the people's search for a viable civilian answer to the military dictatorship. Now that the answer is being muffled, reports have appeared of a revolt in his Peoples' Party in Punjab.[26]

Before the Martial Law was clamped down many West Pakistani leaders had pleaded for a negotiated settlement with

24. *Pakistan Times*, Lahore, 30 April, 1971.
25. *Newskeek*, New York, 10 May, 1971.
26. *Imroze*, Lahore, 4 May, 1971.

Sheikh Mujibur Rehman. Leaders like Air Marshal Nur Khan of the Council Muslim League, Wali Khan of the National Awami Party and Mufti Mehmud of the Jamaat-ul-Ulema had strongly denounced Bhutto for his campaign against the people of East Pakistan. Air Marshal Nur Khan had gone to the extent of saying that Mujibur Rehman's six-point programme of autonomy could be as beneficial for Punjab as for East Bengal. The fact that the Council Muslim League is known to be a rightist party, wedded to the ideals of unity and integrity of Pakistan and is also the second largest political group in Punjab, lends special significance to such pronouncements.

Leaders of the smaller provinces, especially of Baluchistan and NWFP, have always been enthusiastic supporters of the idea of a loose federation which Sheikh Mujibur Rehman was propounding before his arrest. Only a day before war was declared on East Bengal, Wali Khan, the leader of the majority party in Baluchistan and NWFP, met Sheikh Mujibur Rehman and assured him of his full support. His present silence can only be attributed to the reign of terror which the Martial Law has imposed.

Recently there has been a great deal of rethinking among West Pakistani intellectuals about Pakistan's position in southern Asia. They have been suggesting that West Pakistan should dissociate itself from South-East Asia and link up with the West Asian region. Such trends of thought are likely to be strengthened in case the army gets bogged down in the marshes of East Bengal.[27]

But this is no answer to the very deep seated crisis of identity which faces the military regime even in West Pakistan terms. The regime has an extremely narrow socio-economic base. Unlike the Ayub regime, the present ruling elite is not identified with the most powerful province in West Pakistan, the Punjab. Among the dozen most important officers of the military establishment, hardly one-fourth are Punjabis. Barring the air force, no service is headed by an officer from the Punjab. The Punjabis point out with vehemence that neither General Yahya Khan, nor Bhutto and not even General Tikka Khan is a Punjabi. While Bhutto is a Sindi of Kutch origin, Yahya Khan

27. Of special significance is the report of a seminar held by Thinkers' Forum, Lahore, and published in the form of a pamphlet in Urdu. Lahore October, 1970.

is a Persian speaking Pathan and Tikka Khan a Pushtu speaking Pathan. Also both Bhutto and Yahya Khan belong to the minority Shia sect, as did Mohammed Ali Jinnah, while most of the Punjabis are Sunnis. Punjab's share in the army and the civil service is far less than that of other West Pakistani people.

Pakistan newspaper reports indicate a very poor response in the Punjab to recent recruitment drives by the military. The people apparently do not consider military service attractive enough to offer themselves as mercenaries. Reports by Pakistani experts in recent years have continuously talked about the lack of enthusiasm among educated youth of the Punjab to join the officer corps of the defence services. This in turn explains the apathy with which the Punjabis, hitherto regarded as the back-bone of West Pakistani establishment, view President Yahya Khan's war. Punjabi intellectuals have been at pains to explain that the economy of West Pakistan is not in the hands of Punjabis. Out of the 22 top most industrial families who are known to control 70 per cent of Pakistan's organised economic resources, only two are Punjabi. Names like the Ispahanis, Haroons, Adamjees and Daud Seths who have dominated the economic horizon of East Bengal have nothing to do with the Punjab. The fact that Punjabi prosperity is attributed to agriculture and small-scale industries has further convinced the common man in Lahore and Rawalpindi that General Yahya Khan was not fighting his war. Most of the scions of big business houses belong to the Bohra, Memon and Kachi families who had originally migrated from Bombay to Karachi. Some others like the famous Haroons are of Sindhi origin.

The fact that most of the army officers are Pathans has not been much of an advantage for the establishment even in NWFP. Pathan sentiment for regional autonomy has been so strong that the composition of the central leadership would hardly make a material difference. This also explains persistent rumours about the existence of a group of powerful military officers who would like to elbow out General Yahya Khan on one pretext or another. The association of Bhutto's name with some of the potent trouble makers in the army, lends ominous significance to reports that a coup was round the counter when General Yahya Khan was forced to declare war on East Bengal. Failure of the adventure in the East, or even a military stalemate, could mean political upheaval in West Pakistan.

APPENDIX

APPENDIX

CONFLICT IN EAST PAKISTAN

EDWARD S. MASON
ROBERT DORFMAN
STEPHEN A. MARGLIN

Summary

THE INDEPENDENCE of East Pakistan is inevitable. What started as a movement for economic autonomy within the framework of a united Pakistan
has been irrevocably transformed by the wholesale slaughter of East
Pakistani civilians into a movement that sooner or later will produce an
independent East Pakistan—"Bangla Desh" is a matter of time. A complete discussion of the Pakistani question would include an analysis of
cultural, linguistic, and social issues, which along with economics and
politics, are at the heart of the present conflict. This paper has à more
limited goal: to assess the economic and political bases of disaffection in
East Pakistan and to suggest the likely implications for international
relations of the break-up of Pakistan.

In brief, the fact of a large and widening gap in the average standard
of living between the two regions of the country is incontestable. Even
the West Pakistani-dominated Government admits that the average East
Pakistani must make do with barely two-thirds the average income in
the West, and he faces higher prices too. The East Pakistanis argue that
income disparity is largely the result of a systematic subordination of the
interests of the Eastern region to those of the West; specifically, the East
Pakistanis charge that allocation of foreign exchange—both that earned
by the export of East Pakistani jute and that provided by foreign aid—
disproportionately favours West Pakistan; that allocation of domestic investment reinforces the income disparity; and that high tariffs and import

151

quotas raise prices to East Pakistanis in order to provide profits and jobs in West Pakistan.

We believe that in the main the facts support these charges. Pakistan Government policies have at the very least exacerbated the inequalities that arise from an uneven distribution of natural resources between the two regions, and a disproportionate share of the benefits of economic development have accrued to West Pakistan.

The political program of Sheikh Mujib's Awami League, overwhelmingly endorsed by the people of East Pakistan in the recent elections, sought to correct these disparities by transferring control over economic policy from the Central Government to the provinces. The response of the Yahya Khan's Government has been to unleash a reign of terror whose full dimensions are only gradually becoming known.

The West Pakistani Army can delay independence, but terrain and logistics, coupled with the implacable hostility of the East Pakistanis to what has become foreign domination, are on the side of "Bangla Desh". Apart from the elementary and overwhelming humanitarian interest in an end to further bloodshed, American interest lies with a quick rather than a slow realization of independence. Most important, tensions in South Asia will be reduced. Bangla Desh and India will develop mutually advantageous economic and cultural relations, a move long desired by both sides but frustrated by West Pakistanis who have refused to countenance any normalization of relations in the East as long as the Kashmir issue remains outstanding. The Kashmir issue too is likely to subside in importance, not because of any reduction in tension in the West— the Kashmir issue has never aroused much interest in the East— but because West Pakistan, without the economic support of the East, will be unable to sustain the level of pressure it has been able to mount until now. In short, Bangla Desh will be a truly independent state, ready and able to maintain normal relations with its neighbours and the powerful nations of both blocs, but a satellite or pawn of no one.

The independence of Bangla Desh will be inimical to American interests only insofar as American aid is used to delay the inevitable. Economic aid to the Pakistan Government should be immediately suspended. The "one-time" exception made last year to the embargo of arms sales and military aid (imposed after the Indo-Pakistani war of 1965) should be rescinded. American arms must not be supplied to a government that makes war on helpless civilians.

U.S. Aid

Since 1951 Pakistan has been a major recipient of U.S. economic aid amounting to approximately $3 billion[1] by 1969. Except for food aid donated under Public Law 480, the bulk of this assistance has been used

1. Stern, J. J. and Falcon, W. P., *Growth and Development in Pakistan 1955-69*, Occasional Paper No. 23, Harvard Center for International Affairs, April 1970; M. A. Sattar, *United States Aid and Pakistan's Economic Development*, unpublished Ph.D. dissertation, Tufts University, 1969.

to support industrialization in West Pakistan, with only a handful of projects undertaken in East Pakistan.

The quantum of U.S. military aid to Pakistan is a classified figure but two estimates[2] put it between $1.5 to $2 billion for the period between 1954 and 1965. The assistance has included F-104 Starfighters, Patton tanks, armoured personnel carriers, automatic and recoilless infantry weapons. This impressive array of modern weaponry was given expressly[3] for defensive purposes. With Pakistan an early member of SEATO and CENTO this military aid was intended to bolster the armed containment of the Communist Bloc in the Dulles era of U.S. foreign policy but apart from the brief border war with India of 1965 the only active use of these sophisticated weapons has occured against the unarmed and defenseless civilian population of East Pakistan.[4]

The growth and maintenance of the superstructure of the armed forces which was built up with massive U.S. military aid continued even after 1965 when the United States decided to put an embargo on the delivery of arms to both Pakistan and India. This was made possible by diverting resources from the much needed development projects. East Pakistan, poorer and less powerful politically than the West, suffered more by this irrational policy.

Surprisingly, the United States has just recently (October 1970) made an exception to its embargo on military sales to Pakistan. According to the information available, the United States has offered to supply Pakistan the following items:

    (a) Armoured personnel carriers (approximately 300)

    (b) Maritime reconnaissance aircraft (4)

    (c) F-104 jet fighters (6)

    (d) B-57 bombers (7)

Fortunately, no sales or deliveries have yet been made. It is not too late to rescind the offer, a move that would be of practical as well as symbolic value.

Disparities

The basic facts seem to support the East Pakistan charge of economic domination by the West. The economic disparities between East and West Pakistan have been so serious for so long that the Pakistan government's highest planning authority has been forced to take official note of them.

A recent report[5] by a panel of experts to The Planning Commission of

2. *New York Times*, September 28, 1964; Frank N. Trager, "United States and Pakistan," *Orbis, Vol.* IX, Fall 1965, No. 3.

3. Formal agreement signed May 1954, reported in Department of State Press release, *Department of State Bulletin*, May 31, 1954, pp. 850-851.

4. *Washington Post*, March 30; *New York Times*, March 29 and March 30. These contain eyewitness accounts by correspondents of use of U.S. supplied tanks.

5. *Reports of the Advisory Panels for the Fourth Five Year Plan 1970-75*, Vol. I; Planning Commission, Government of Pakistan, July, 1970.

the Government of Pakistan provides authoritative documentation of the widening of economic disparities in the two regions. The most striking fact in this report is the widening gap between the income of the average West Pakistani and his Eastern counterpart. In 1959-60, the per capita income in West Pakistan was 32% higher than in the East. Over the next ten years the annual rate of growth of income of West Pakistan was 6.2% while it was only 4.2% in East Pakistan. As a result, by 1969-70 the per capita income of the West was 61% higher than in the East.[6] Thus in ten years the income gap doubled in percentage terms; it increased even more in absolute terms.

East Pakistanis blame three instruments of central government policy for their plight:

1. Pakistan's scant investible resources, plus foreign aid, are directed unduly to the development of West Pakistan—to the comparative neglect of East Pakistan.

2. In particular, East Pakistan's foreign trade earnings are diverted to finance imports for West Pakistan.

3. Economic policy favours West Pakistan at the expense of the East. Specifically, tariffs, import controls, and industrial licensing compel East Pakistan to purchase commodities from West Pakistan which, but for the controls, they could obtain more cheaply in world markets.

We believe the East Pakistani claims to be largely justified. First, it is indisputable that the bulk of public investment has been in West Pakistan though the majority of the population lies in the East. With 60% of the population, East Pakistan's share of central government development expenditure has been as low as 20% during 1950/51-1954/55, attaining a peak of 36% during the Third Five Year Plan period 1965/66-1969/70. East Pakistan has received an even smaller share of private investment, less than 25%.[7]

It may be true, as defenders of Pakistan government policy claim, that the great bulk of worthwhile investment opportunities have been in the West, though the relative attractiveness of the West may be more the effect of overall government policy than a cause. In any event the fact remains that investments in the West have done little or nothing for the people in the East.

As for the second point, it is clear that foreign exchange has been allocated to the detriment of East Pakistan. Over the last two decades East Pakistan's share of total Pakistan export earnings has varied between 50% and 70%, while its share of imports has been in the range of 25% to 30%.[8] Until 1962/63 East Pakistan has shown significant sur-

6. *Ibid.,* p. 2, Table 1. As the report notes these estimates of disparity are understatements because of a lack of adjustment in the basic official data for the generally higher prices which prevail in East compared to West.

7. *Ibid.,* p. 6, table 2.

8. Total foreign exchange available for imports is made up of export earnings and foreign aid. All data on trade are compiled from official statistics issued by the Central Statistical Office, Government of Pakistan.

pluses on foreign account, which has changed in recent years to small deficits. By contrast the West's foreign trade has shown a substantial and chronic deficit that has absorbed virtually all foreign exchange made available through foreign aid.

With respect to the third point, general economic policy has clearly favoured West Pakistan. The West's preponderant share of imports and investments might have provided inexpensive necessities for all of Pakistan's people. In fact it has allowed the development of inefficient[9] industries, which, ironically, have prospered largely because of tariffs and quotas that have made East Pakistan a captive market. 40% of all exports of West Pakistan are sold to East Pakistan; in 1968/69 the West sold 50% more to the East than it bought from the East.

An analysis of foreign trade data reveals that a net transfer of resources has taken place from East to West Pakistan. According to the official report referred to above, East Pakistan has transferred approximately $2.6 billion to West Pakistan over the period 1948/49 to 1968/69.[10]

In short, Pakistan's economic policies are harmful to East Pakistan. "Exploitation" may be a strong word, but it seems clear, all in all, that East Pakistan's economic interests have been subordinated to those of the West, and that the East Pakistanis have had good cause to resent that fact.

The economic domination of East Pakistan has been facilitated by West Pakistani dominance of the Central Government. The military regime in Pakistan has existed, with modifications, since 1958, and decision-making authority rests with a well-entrenched civil service and their military bosses. *All* senior military members of the administration have been West Pakistani, and of the senior officers in the Central civil services, 87% were West Pakistani in 1960,[11] and the proportion has not changed much since. The Deputy Chairman of the Planning Commission and the Central Finance Minister, key individuals in resource allocation, have always been West Pakistanis.

The location of the Central Government in West Pakistan has encouraged the concentration of industry and the entrepreneurial class in West Pakistan.[12] Such a concentration is to be expected in an economic system where direct allocational control of resources by the government makes direct access to government authorities a prime business asset.

Background

The history of economic and political domination of East Pakistan by

9. Lewis, Stephen R., *Pakistan: Industrialization and Trade Policies,* O.E.C.D., Oxford University Press, 1970.

10. Planning Commission, *op. cit.,* appendix 3.

11. Rahman, A., *East and West Pakistan: A Problem in Political Economy of Regional Planning,* Occasional Paper No. 20, Harvard University Center for International Affairs, 1968. By 1966, among all Class 1 officers in the Central Government East Pakistan's share was only 20 per cent.

12. Papanek, G. F., *Pakistan's Development: Social Goals and Private Inventives,* Harvard University Press, 1967.

the West led naturally to increasing demands for provincial autonomy, spearheaded by Sheikh Mujibur Rahman's Awami League. Its 6-point platform for autonomy sought to transfer control over foreign trade, foreign aid allocation, and taxation powers to the provinces so that no province could be dominated through disproportionate control of the Central Government's powers over resource allocation.[13]

At the polls last December this Awami League platform swept 167 of the 169 seats in the National Constitutional Assembly that were allotted to East Pakistan. The Awami League's 167 seats constituted an absolute majority in a chamber of 313. The political and military powers of West Pakistan tried to pressure Sheikh Mujib into compromising on his 6-point autonomy mandate. In particular Zulfikar Alí Bhutto, leader of the West Pakistani People's Party which had won 80-odd seats in the elections, demanded that control of trade and aid should remain with the Central Government. When Sheikh Mujib refused to compromise on these instruments of past economic domination, Bhutto announced a boycott of the Constitutional Assembly scheduled to meet on March 3. General Yahya Khan used this pretext to postpone the Assembly indefinitely. This arbitary postponement provoked demonstrations in Dacca and other cities on March 1, which the military decided to control by force. The military authorities conceded 172 deaths in the disturbances (the Dacca correspondent to the *London Observer* put the figure nearer 2000). Despite this bloody provocation the Awami League refrained from declaring independence. Instead they launched a campaign of civil disobedience to demand a return of troops to barracks and an enquiry into the firings. The campaign of non-cooperation effectively transferred civilian authority to Sheikh Mujib but even in the massive rally of March 7 Sheikh Mujib still spoke of a united Pakistan with autonomy for each province. His preparedness for negotiation and commitment to the unity of Pakistan was demonstrated by his continuation of talks for the next two weeks despite the well-advertised influx of West Pakistani troops. Indeed, in retrospect it would appear that the West Pakistani officials were never negotiating in good faith; negotiations were a way to forestall an open break until sufficient numbers of West Pakistani troops could be brought on the scene to unleash a terror whose full dimensions are only now becoming known. The Awami League's commitment to a peaceful political settlement was convincingly demonstrated

---

13. The Six Points are:

(1) Establishment of a federation "on the basis of the Lahore Resolution and the Parliamentary framework of government with supremacy of legislature directly elected on the basis of adult franchise."

(2) Federal government shall deal with only two subjects, that is, defense and foreign affairs, and all other residuary subjects should rest in the federating states.

(3) There should be either two separate but freely convertible currencies for the two wings or one currency for the whole country provided that effective constitutional provisions were made to stop the flight of capital from East to West Pakistan. There should be separate banking

by the complete lack of preparation of the civilian population to the onslaught[14] of military arms which was unleashed on them on the night of Thursday, March 25.

Implications

From news reports now available it would appear that the use of massive military fire power has broken the Awami League and its supporters in most urban centers. But control of urban centers at gunpoint in a country where 90% of the population lives in rural areas hardly constitutes a framework for any effective government, let alone a popular one. The immediate prospect is for ruthless military rule in urban centers, with tenuous control over a countryside which is likely to become increasingly the base for armed guerilla resistance.

The base for such a movement clearly exists. The overwhelming support for the Awami League's demand for autonomy was clearly shown in the election results of December when 167 out of 169 seats allocated to East Pakistan were won by the League. As reports of military massacres[15] are carried by urban refugees to the rural areas, the democratically expressed sentiment for autonomy is likely to be converted to a militant desire for independence. It is possible that a West Pakistani army of occupation can suppress the Bengali nation for two months, six months, or a year, but the American experience in Vietnam illustrates only too painfully the impossibility of holding an entire population captive by force of alien arms alone.

The emergence of an independent Bangla Desh appears to be inevitable

---

reserves and separate fiscal and monetary policy for East Pakistan.

(4) Denial to the Central Government of the right of taxation; vesting of tax provisions in the hands of the federating states with the Central Government receiving a fixed share.

(5) Foreign trade; Five steps shall be taken:

    (a) There shall be two separate accounts for foreign exchange earnings.

    (b) Earnings of East Pakistan shall be under the control of East Pakistan and the same for West Pakistan.

    (c) Foreign exchange requirements of the federal government shall be met by the two wings either equally or in a ratio to be fixed.

    (d) Indigenous products shall move free of duty within the two wings.

    (e) The constitution shall empower the unit governments to establish trade and commercial relations with, set up trade missions in and enter into agreements with foreign countries.

(6) Set up a militia or para military force by East Pakistan.

14. Preplanned according to reports by foreign correspondents, e.g. Sydney Schanberg in *New York Times,* March 26-29.

15. The eyewitness account of a British correspondent in *Washington Post,* March 30 leaves no doubt about the appropriateness of the word "massacre".

in the long run. What remains in question is how much blood will flow before it occurs. Politically it is clear that the longer it takes to achieve independence, the more likely it is that control of the independence movement will slip away from the moderate leadership of the Awami League to the more leftist National Awami Party (which did not contest the December elections).

Assuming that the independence movement succeeds while under Awami League control, certain predictions may be made about its relations with neighbours and super-powers. As expressed in public statements of Sheikh Mujib, an independent Bangla Desh will establish friendly relations with India and set up economic trade to their mutual advantage. Up to now such trade—and all cultural ties have been frustrated by the West Pakistanis who dominated the Central Government. They believe that, short of war, their only lever to force a settlement of their Kashmir claim is the economic interest of India in trade with East Pakistan. By contrast, East Pakistan has never been aroused by Kashmir, and in the 1965 war no military activity took place within its borders. Strong linguistic and cultural ties with the state of West Bengal in India are likely to help cement durable good relations between the two countries and reduce tension in the area. Unable to share the burden of military expenditures with the East, West Pakistan is bound to tone down its policy of confrontation with India, a confrontation which for the past 24 years has diverted scarce resources of both these poor, populous countries from much needed economic development to defense.

As an independent nation Bangla Desh might conceivably establish marginal economic contacts with Communist China. But these are unlikely to be any greater than the current scale of trade and aid between China and Pakistan, and will certainly be less than the likely range and depth of East Bengal's economic ties to neighbouring India. As long as India is the main trading partner (and both pronouncements of Awami League leaders and the economic geography of the region support this possibility), it is unlikely that Bangla Desh will become a satellite of Communist China.

The U.S.S.R. has in the past three years become an active patron of the military clique that controls Pakistan. Soviet aid has included considerable economic aid (including agreements for a steel mill in West Pakistan) and some military aid. The Soviet initiative has been largely a response to growing Communist Chinese ties with Pakistan. This competition between rival giants has redounded to the benefit of West Pakistan where the central government and military establishment are based. The U.S.S.R. has not been sensitive to the aspirations of East Pakistanis in the past, and is unlikely to make a new Bangla Desh an arena for superpower competition for influence.

A major goal of U.S. foreign policy in this area has been the reduction of the debilitating confrontation between India and Pakistan. This goal will surely be advanced by the existence of an independent Bangla Desh friendly to India. Most observers believe that the Awami League leadership will follow a neutral foreign policy, particularly if the U.S. and multilateral aid agencies like the World Bank are the major aid donors.

158

Bengali independence will be inimical to American interests only if by following short-sighted policies we drive East Pakistan into the arms of another power—the U.S.S.R. or China. To the extent that Bengali independence is delayed by means of American arms, the image of the United States will suffer, and rightly so. The offer of arms to Pakistan by the United States Government in October 1970, whatever its ostensible purpose, will, if implemented, oil a Pakistani military machine that is making war on its own citizens. The United States Government must rescind this offer forthwith. No further military aid, or economic aid—which directly or indirectly provides foreign exchange that make it possible to buy weapons abroad—should be given to West Pakistan until it withdraws its occupation force from East Bengal and recognizes the independence of the Bengali nation.

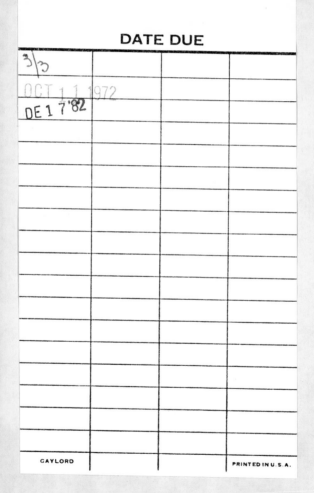

DATE DUE

3/3			
OCT 1 1 1972			
DE 1 7 '82			
GAYLORD			PRINTED IN U.S.A.